FUN THINGS TO DO WITH YOUR KIDS

FUN THINGS TO DO WITH YOUR KIDS

The Family Book of Games, Hobbies, Trips and Activities

by

Carl Dreizler and Phil Phillips

Galahad Books • New York

First Galahad Books edition published in 1995.

Galahad Books
A division of Budget Book Service, Inc.
386 Park Avenue South
New York, NY 10016

Galahad Books is a registered trademark of Budget Book Service, Inc.

Published by arrangement with Thomas Nelson, Inc., Publishers.

Library of Congress Catalog Card Number: 95-75030

ISBN: 0-88365-895-X

Printed in the United States of America.

Contents

I

Just for Fun, Games and Activities

To
Scott, Sonya, Ross, new baby Leif
and a mystery boy or girl
due to arrive soon.
With love from
Uncle Carl.

▲ Contents

▲ Acknowledgments

With deep gratitude I wish to thank *Victor Oliver* for giving me the opportunity to make a lifelong dream of writing books come true; *Lila Empson* for bringing harmony to the words; my *parents* and my *brothers* and *sisters* for helping create many of the memories expressed as ideas in this book; the many *friends* with whom God has blessed me for allowing me the honor of having fun with their children; and very specially *Steve Arterburn* for making the initial introduction to Victor.

▲ Introduction

No one is more important to the world of tomorrow than the children of today. As adults we can offer one great gift to the children in our lives, which will help build their character and demonstrate our love. That gift is our time.

Think back to your own childhood. What are your fondest memories? Going down to the park and riding the merry-go-round with your dad standing beside you? Sitting at the breakfast table as your mom brought you a platter of steaming hot pancakes? Visiting grandma and grandpa on the farm? Or summer camp hikes with the youth pastor from church?

Perhaps you have memories such as these that you would like to pass on to the children in your life. This book suggests many other ways to have fun with your own children. Perhaps some of the ideas listed will bring to mind more of your own precious childhood memories.

On the other hand, you may not have many fond memories of your childhood. This book will provide you with ideas and activities you can use, which may become the cherished memories *your* children will take into their adult years.

The pages that follow contain many ways for you to have fun with the children in your life. Although most of the ideas are appropriate for kids of almost any age, there are examples of activities that are fun for you to do with toddlers, elementary-age children, and even teenagers. As the title indicates, each idea is simple to plan and implement, although some ideas may inspire you to do more planning and preparation.

The book has purposely been written to be useful not only to parents, but to aunts, uncles, grandparents, youth pastors, and friends of children everywhere. Consider the children that are special in your life. Then look through these pages to find the idea that is just right for each child. Next, make a "date" with them. This book stresses the important task of setting up regular dates to have fun with your kids.

Time is one of the most precious gifts anyone could give to another human being. Eventually your children will be grown up and will move away from you. Give them something to take with them: a heart full of happy memories of having fun with you.

1 ▲ Building Blocks

The Idea: Decide on a building project you and your child will do together. It might be something simple like a model airplane with only a few parts to assemble or something more complex like a birdhouse the two of you design and build.

Building Plans: You may already have something in mind for your building project. But just in case you don't, we have provided some ideas to start your planning process.

> *Birdhouse:* You could probably design and build a birdhouse without having specific plans. However, there are books to tell you how to build the right birdhouse for the types of birds in your area. For example, you will want to make the opening large enough for the bird to enter. Yet, it must be small enough to keep predators out. Your house can be as simple as four walls and a roof or as extravagant as a birdhouse done in Tudor-style architecture.

> *Model car or airplane:* If you are not crafty with a saw or other tools, try building a

model car or airplane with your child. There are kits for plastic car models or kits for assembling an airplane from balsa wood complete with fabric to put around the frame.

Pet home: Perhaps you have a dog or cat that needs its own home. Like the birdhouse, you have the option of creating a simple structure or a house that is the same color and design as your own. Then your dog or cat will really feel like a part of the family.

Toy house: Build a toy house with your child. You can either design a custom-built home or purchase books that give you plans for building doll houses of different sizes and shapes.

Soapbox Derby car: Perhaps when you were a child you made a Soapbox Derby car. Help your child build one of his or her own.

Furniture: You may not be able to create furniture suitable for your living room, but perhaps you and your child can build porch furniture or miniature furniture for a doll house.

Bookshelves: One of the other ideas in this book suggests that you start a library for your child. Why not begin that library the right way by building the shelves together?

2 ▲ See 'Em Museum

The Idea: Take your kids to various museums in your area. Not only can this be a fun experience for all of you, but you can learn a great deal, too.

Museum Hopping: There are many different types of museums for you to explore with your kids.

> *Natural history:* Natural history museums are popular among children. It is there, in most cases, that they will be able to see the skeletons of the great beasts that once walked the Earth. In fact, they may be able to see re-creations of scenes showing beasts that still walk the Earth. In addition, if your children are studying the lives of Native Americans or cultures of people in other lands, they will probably be able to see displays of artifacts they have had to learn about only through written or spoken words in school.

> *Science and industry:* While science may be boring to some children, it is equally as fas-

cinating to others. In the science and indus-
try museum located near where I live, there
are displays that allow the observer to learn
principles of physics by pushing buttons or
pulling levers. (Kids love to push buttons
and pull levers.) There are also displays that
simulate an earthquake, explain how the inner ear works, and show what makes a wave
break as it approaches the shore. Other exhibits allow you to see what astronauts see
when they lift off in the space shuttle.

Art: Although art museums may be the favorite type of museum among adults, they
will probably not be your child's first pick.
However, your child may be learning in
school about Van Gogh, Renoir, or Rock-
well. Remember, art does not have to be
boring. Try to find museums that display
comic art or sculptures that might interest
your children.

Specialty museums: There are a great variety
of specialty museums. Your child may be
fascinated by space travel. If you're in Wash-
ington D.C., a visit to the Air and Space
Museum is a must. Maybe your kid loves
cowboys. Visit the Cowboy Museum in
Oklahoma City. Race cars? Visit the Indianapolis 500 Museum on the track's infield.
There are toy museums, train museums,

movie museums, doll museums. The options are almost unlimited.

Record Your Museum Visits: Keep this book handy so that you can write down the various types of museums you visit in your city and state. Try to take your kids to see all of them over the next year or so.

Museums Visitation Record		
TYPE OF MUSEUM	LOCATION	DATE
_____	_____	_____
_____	_____	_____
_____	_____	_____
_____	_____	_____
_____	_____	_____
_____	_____	_____
_____	_____	_____
_____	_____	_____
_____	_____	_____
_____	_____	_____

3 ▲ Name of the Game

The Idea: Once in awhile, when the kids are playing games like hide-and-seek or tag, ask if you can play with them. You may find it a humbling experience, but the neighbor kids will go home asking their parents, "How come you never play hide-and-seek with me? Sonya's parents do."

Games People Play (Outdoors): When the weather is nice, teach your kids to play games outdoors. Hide-and-seek and tag are probably already on their list of games to play. If they don't know some of the games you played as a child, take some time to teach them the rules. Here are a few suggestions:

> *Kick-the-can:* While everyone probably has his own rules to kick-the-can, this game can be played by forming two teams. Members of team one hide in various places within specified boundaries. Everyone in team two tries to find them. If a member of team one is caught by a member of team two, he or she is taken to a home base. If all members of team one are found, team two wins and

takes its turn hiding in the next round of play. At any time during the game, if a member of the team in hiding is able to run to a central location and kick a tin can without being caught, all members of the team are "free," and that team wins. The winning team becomes the team in hiding during the next round.

Hopscotch: Maybe a few kids still play hopscotch today, but if yours don't, teach them how. You'll have to have someone show you the diagram of a hopscotch course, if you have forgotten. The object is to go up and back upon the diagram,

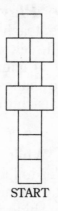

START

jumping with one foot in each square and moving your laggard through the squares. You cannot jump in a square that contains your opponents laggard. If this description has you baffled, find an old hopscotch expert and he or she will show you how to play.

Three-flies-up: Three-flies-up can be played with a Frisbee, bat and ball, football, or any other object that is normally thrown. One person hits or tosses the object into a crowd. The first person who catches the object three times gets to be the next one to hit or toss it to the others.

Games People Play (Indoors): When the weather gets bad outside or when the kids are in an indoor-playing-mood, you can come through with some of the games you played as a child. Here are our suggestions. Some may be new to you, and others are listed to jog your memory.

Sardines: Looking for a game the entire family, youth group, or slumber party gang can play? Try Sardines! This game is best played on a dark night when little or no moonlight or city lights shine into your home. Begin by turning off every light in the house. Then everyone stays in a particular room while the person who is "it" hides somewhere else in the house. No one can talk or ask questions. The object of the game? To find the hiding person and hide with him or her. Once everyone has found the missing person and hides in the same place, that round is over. Just try playing this game without laughing.

Board games: The list of board games is almost unlimited. Try the old favorites like Scrabble or Monopoly, or the more modern Trivial Pursuit.

Card games: If you come from a family that played lots of cards, you no doubt will pass that pastime on to your children. Could it be that avid card playing is hereditary? Find out if your children know how to play these favorite card games:

- Fish
- Concentration
- Hearts
- Crazy eights
- Authors
- Uno

4 ▲ Pitter Patter

The Idea: Next time it rains on a day when you are with the kids, try diverting from the traditional rule of "You can't go outside because you'll get wet." Here are some ways to have fun both indoors and outdoors when it rains.

A Splash of Fun: As responsible adults we know that the best thing for kids during a downpour is to keep them inside, dry and warm. While I certainly wouldn't want to encourage starting any bad habits, I think that rain can be a good setting for fun. Here are some outdoor opportunities for you to have fun with your kids during a rain shower (you can even use this time to teach your child about road safety and watching for cars):

> *Puddle splashing:* Bundle up in warm clothes and cover yourselves with as many waterproof garments as you can: raincoats, hats, and galoshes. Then go outside and find puddles to jump in. Your kids may be shocked at your behavior, and your neighbors may think you've completely gone off

your rocker, but you will have the time of your life with the kids.

Sing: As you walk along the street with your child, try to think about songs that mention rain. Sing each song as you think of it.

Boat in the gutter: Find a cork or some other object that will float, and drop it into the rushing water in a gutter. Follow it for as long as you can. You and your child can make up stories about the object as it moves from one "adventure" to another.

Find shelter: If the rain becomes drenching, find a safe place to stand and watch (remember safety rules concerning electrical storms, of course). Though you may not stay dry, you and your child can look all around and see just how beautiful a rainstorm can be.

Play football: Football in the rain? The pros do it. Why can't you and your kids? Find a muddy playing field. Assuming that you're wearing old clothes, play a game of tackle football and roll around in the mud. Remember, the point of this activity is to have fun—not to stay clean.

Mud pies: Did you ever make mud pies as a kid? Did you decorate the top of the pies with daisy petals or dandelions? Well, here's your chance to teach the kids all your techniques. Bring out some old aluminum pie tins from the kitchen. While the mud is still wet, have everyone make a mud pie.

The Inside Scoop: After you're done with your wet outdoor excursion, bring the kids back inside. Make hot cocoa, change into dry clothes, and sit in front of a warm, cozy fire. Then consider some activities that you can do indoors when the storm is too fierce to go outside.

Games: Consider playing your favorite card games or board games.

Watch the storm: Look out the window and watch the storm. If there is lightning, count the seconds until you hear the thunder.

Jigsaw puzzle: There is no better time to get out a jigsaw puzzle and put it together as a group than when the wind is howling, the rain is falling, and the firewood is burning. Assemble the puzzle while listening to your favorite relaxing music.

Use this book: When the storms come along, pull this book off the shelf and consider the other ideas in the book that are indoor activities, such as baking, making crafts, or putting together a family album.

5 ▲ Story Time

The Idea: There are lots of ways to tell your kids a story besides picking up a book and reading it to them. Try writing a story of your own, or let them help you create a story.

Write a Fairy Tale: If you're saying, "Me? Write a fairy tale? Why I've never written a thing in my life." Nonsense! You can do it. Write one about your child. Sit down with a pad of paper some day when the house is quiet, and see how much you can do. All you need are some main characters (the people in your family or youth group), a location (your home town), and a plot (pick some dilemma your child is facing).

For example, if you live in the mountains of Colorado, and your child missed the goal for what could have been the winning point in a soccer game, your fairy tale might go something like this:

> Once upon a time a pretty little girl named Sally lived in a magical place high upon a hill. She had hair that shined like the sun off a still pond and cute little freckles all over her face.

All around her house were trees that always made everything smell good. The trees seemed to reach higher than the clouds. Sally would spend hours each day talking to her friends, Sandy Squirrel and Randy Raccoon, who lived in these trees.

When Sally wasn't home playing with her friends, she was either in school learning about the world beyond her little village, or she was playing games in Mountain Meadow with other little girls and boys.

One day Sally was sad because she didn't kick the checkerboard ball through the candy cane poles. As she sat beneath one of the great trees in her back yard, Sandy Squirrel came up to talk with her.

"What's wrong," Sandy asked. "You look so sad."

"Oh, I let my team down today when we were playing on Mountain Meadow. We lost the game, and it's my fault."

"Sally, did you try your best?"

"Yes," Sally said with a whimper.

"Well, honey, if you go through life always trying to do your best, you will never have to be ashamed of the outcome. It's okay to be sad sometimes, but always try to pick yourself up again and move onward. Here's an acorn I collected today. Keep it with you. Whenever you feel sad or defeated, hold on to the acorn and remember our little talk we had today. You will never let me down, if you just keep trying to do your best."

Sally took the acorn from Sandy Squirrel and placed it in a secret place so that she could always find it and remember their little talk.

"Thank you, Sandy," Sally said with a smile. "It's already working. I'm not so sad anymore. See you tomorrow."

"Bye my friend," Sandy Squirrel said, and she scampered off to her home in the trees.

In this abbreviated example the mother or father reading the story might hand Sally an acorn so that she can save it to remind her of the story. It's really not that difficult to write a simple story like this. Just allow the little child within you to create the story.

Fill in the Blanks: Another option is to make up a story on the spot. In this case you can have the child help you by filling in the blank each time you pause. For example, you might begin, "Once upon a time there was a little . . ." And your child might say, ". . . turtle." Then you might say, "And the turtle's name was . . ." And your child might say, ". . . Roscoe."

Continue building the story in this way. Don't worry about the plot making any sense. You and your child will have so much fun making up sentences and filling in the blanks that your story can be just as silly and nonsensical as possible.

6 ▲ Fort Ordinary

The Idea: Help your kids build a fort or other hideaway where they can play during the day and even sleep during the night.

Building Your Hideaway: To implement this idea you can be as simple or as creative as you want. Some of the following suggestions can take place on the spur of the moment, while others will require some time and materials to complete. In any case, this way to have fun may teach your child how to be resourceful by using simple objects to create special memories.

Here are a few ways to create special hideaways.

Living room fortress: Help your kids create a fortress right in your own living room or family room. This idea is particularly handy when the weather is cold or wet outside, and the kids are getting cabin fever from staying indoors. Use common everyday things around the house to create your fun fort.

For example, begin by placing two card tables end to end. Then take two or three very large bedspreads and place them over the tables so that the edges of the bedspreads touch the floor. To create more room inside the fortress, pull the ends of the bedspreads along the floor as far away from the tables as possible, and then hold them in place by putting books or other objects on top of the corners.

Your kids should have a fairly spacious hiding place for escaping into their own world. They may want to designate certain parts of their fortress as various rooms. Let them sleep there one night. Once you help them build it, their imaginations will take care of the rest.

Backyard tent: Do you rarely go on camping trips because there never seems to be enough time or because the preparation for such trips always seems so grueling? Don't deprive your kids of such experiences. Help them set up a tent in their own backyard!

Help the kids experience a camping trip by assembling a tent together, eating your meals there, and even sleeping there if the weather permits.

Tree house: If you are fortunate enough to have a large tree on your property, and your kids are old enough to use it safely, why not help your kids create a tree house?

There are few hiding places more private and more memorable to a child than a home in the trees. I won't provide plans for your tree house. That part is up to you and the shape of your tree.

Playhouse: If you are blessed with carpentry skills but are not able to build a tree house, perhaps you could build a small playhouse for your children. You can make it as simple as a one-room home or get more extravagant and include a kitchen, living room, and dining area. If you are not able to build a permanent playhouse, try creating one out of old refrigerator cartons and other large cardboard boxes.

Clubhouse: Did you ever watch "The Li'l Rascals" when you were a little rascal yourself? What a great show. We always wondered how those kids could have such a great clubhouse for their meetings and shows. Perhaps you could help your kids find a place where they, too, can start a neighborhood club. Maybe you or one of the neighbors has an old woodshed that could be converted. Perhaps you could section off a corner of the garage for them. Maybe one of the neighborhood parents has already built a playhouse like the one suggested above.

Your kids' lives can be greatly enhanced if they see you are interested in helping them create fun for themselves and their friends. Maybe they'll even name the club after you!

7 ▲ Growing Up

The Idea: Teach your children about the process of growing up by planting a garden or tree in your yard or somewhere in your city.

Planting: As you first begin to consider this idea with your child, review some of the following options to see which seem most exciting (or practical) for everyone involved.

> A *flower garden:* Perhaps your child will want to plant a garden that will bring forth many colorful spring flowers. This can be an educational experience as well as a fun experience as you examine and study the different types of bulbs and seeds and then watch them as they begin to grow.
> You might consider creating signs for your garden (or a map) so that you know which flowers are sprouting as they begin to break through the ground.
>
> A *vegetable garden:* Your kid is not eating vegetables? If your child takes the time to plant, water, and nurture a garden full of

various vegetables, you might just get him or her to try eating some of the produce.

A tree: Perhaps you don't have the time or the space to create a garden near your home. So plant a tree somewhere nearby. There may be a park near your home, or a place along the highway, where the city will allow you to plant your very own tree. Then your children can watch the progress of the tree that was planted when they were little.

Growing Lessons: You can use the experience of growing plants to help your kids learn lots of different concepts. For example, perhaps your son is in junior high school. All the other boys have started growing tall, but he is still quite short. Perhaps you could show him how the ivy on a wall grows so quickly you can't seem to stop it, but the big oak tree took many years to grow to its stature and strength. Help him realize that he may grow at a later age, or that he may never grow as tall as his friends. Explain that this doesn't mean he won't become a man of great internal or external strength some day.

Growth chart: When your kids are little, start a growth chart somewhere in your home for each child, tracking the date and their height at various times throughout the year. Perhaps you could use one of the door frames.

8 ▲ A Horse Is a Horse, Of Course, Of Course

The Idea: Almost all kids like horses. Why not take your kids out for a morning or afternoon excursion to locations where they can find these pretty animals?

Horse Play: There are many different places where you can take the kids in order to view, pet, or ride horses. The following are a few of the possibilities you may consider.

> *Amusement park:* In many cities there are small amusement parks that offer pony rides for children.

> *Stables:* Not far from where I grew up was a large stable where horses were boarded and kept. We knew it simply as the red barn. Children loved to go there and see the horses. Perhaps there's a place near you like that, a place where you can take the kids and watch the owners train their horses. If you ask, some people may even let your kids brush or pet the horse.

Rodeo: If your child is a horse lover, take him or her to the rodeo. You'll see horses of many kinds there, including bucking broncos. Perhaps you can watch trick riders and really give the kids a thrill.

Horse shows: Find out when there is going to be a horse show near you. You can probably research this by calling nearby boarding stables. If they do not have horse shows themselves, they may be able to direct you to the nearest show.

Polo game: Most of us think we'd have to travel to England to see a polo match. However, there are plenty of polo games played in the United States. You may have to search for a while to find them, but a local university near you may know about polo matches in your area.

Horseback riding: Maybe your kids are too old to ride ponies. In that case take them out for a horseback ride on a full-grown horse. Some places allow you to take the horse anywhere you want to go, but in most cases you will need to go with a guide.

9 ▲ And the Band Played On

The Idea: Make it a habit of taking your kids to various parades in your town or towns near you.

Parade Hits: You can be sure of one thing when it comes to parades. No two are ever alike. Parades are held for many different reasons. Try to find as much variety as possible. When you've seen one parade, you *haven't* seen them all. Here are just a few types of parades you may have the opportunity to see with your kids. See how many parades you can go to in one year!

> *Hometown parade:* Your hometown may have an annual parade celebrating the date of its founding or some other significant event.

> *Holiday parade:* Perhaps the biggest time of year for parades is the Christmas holidays. However, there are often parades celebrating other holidays, such as the Fourth of July, Thanksgiving, and Easter.

> *The biggies:* If your house isn't along the route of one of the nationally-famous pa-

rades of the year (such as the Tournament of Roses in Pasadena), you should consider planning a trip with your kids to see one of them.

Armed Forces Day: In some cities, there are large parades on Armed Forces Day. On other occasions, such as Veterans Day, there are also parades featuring various military groups.

Ticker tape: Unless you live in New York City or some other major metropolitan area, you have probably never been to a ticker tape parade. Perhaps, however, you can attend a similar parade in a city near you when it honors someone or some group, such as a major league baseball team that has just won the World Series.

Boat parade: If you live anywhere near water, you may get to see a boat parade. Some marinas have Christmas boat parades, wooden ship parades, and other events, such as one celebrating the opening of yachting season.

Reign on Your Own Parade: Perhaps

there aren't many parades near your town or city. It doesn't have to be that way. Consider starting a tradition in your city. Get a group together and organize a parade celebrating an event or anniversary. The parade might celebrate something that is unique to your area, "The Fig Harvest Parade" or "The Prairie Dog Festival," for example.

To make it simple, help your kids organize a parade just for all the people on your block or in your section of the city. Set a date. Pass out flyers. Encourage people to dress up, play instruments, or do anything else that seems like fun. Then invite the neighbors from nearby blocks (and the press!) to come and watch you and your friends walk down the sidewalk. Like we said. No two parades are alike. Yours will have a uniqueness all its own.

10 ▲ Hearts and Crafts

The Idea: Spend time with your kids doing creative arts and crafts. Are the kids going to see grandma soon? Help them make her something. Or, have them make something that you will deliver together to a lonely person in your neighborhood or in a nearby nursing home.

Arts and Craft Ideas: There could easily be a book entitled *Simple Arts and Crafts to Share with Your Children*. Here are a few ideas to get you started until such a book appears.

> *Knitting:* My grandmother was a master at knitting. Every time she made a sweater for me I considered it an honor. I still treasure each one. And now, because my grandmother shared this craft with her daughter, my mother knits. If you are a master seamstress or knitter, pass your skill along to your child. You may knit more than just a sweater; you may knit together your relationship.

Stamping: One of the fastest growing arts and crafts ideas is that of rubber stamping. A wide variety of stamps are available. Recently there was a rubber stamp convention near my home. A friend attended to obtain more stamps for her rapidly expanding collection. She is truly a master of the craft. Together with your child you can create birthday cards, party invitations, flyers, and newsletters.

Clay or Play-Doh: Depending on the age of your child, and their level of expertise as a sculptor, you can spend time molding objects out of Play-Doh, or you might purchase some modeling clay for more elaborate sculptures.

Woodworking: Perhaps you are a master at working with wood. As soon as your child is old enough, you may want to begin including him or her in your woodworking projects. Although you may not want to allow the child to use the electric saw, he or she can help assemble the item.

Painting: There are a lot of options with regard to painting. You can fingerpaint together, use water colors, or buy a Paint-By-Number kit.

You know much better than anyone what your special artistic skills are. You might also have some ideas for a new craft you'd like to learn. Perhaps origami (paper folding) has always interested you.

11 ▲ Moving Pictures

The Idea: Have your child help you assemble and create albums from the family pictures you have taken. They can help you write captions or think of creative ways to display the photos. When you're done displaying the still pictures, create some new memories by making a family or group movie together.

The Family Album: Perhaps your family pictures are in a box with no order and no indication of time, persons shown, or specific events. If one of your projects is to get the family pictures organized, ask your kids to help.

You can almost make it a game. Ask the kids to arrange all the pictures based on how old they look. If you really want to make it more fun, include the pictures from your younger days, and see if they are able to tell which of your pictures are the oldest.

Once you have arranged all the photos, begin filling albums in a chronological order or use a different album to feature each person of the family. As you assemble the albums, ask your children to think of captions for some of the photos. Their ideas will probably surprise and delight you.

Photo Shoot: Spend an afternoon taking pictures together. Pick a theme. For example, you may want to go out and take pictures of wildflowers in the desert, or pictures of people in the park. Or you may focus on anything that is old. Once each person has finished taking pictures, have them developed and share them with one another.

Family Movies: Set a time to get out the old family movies. If you have any eight millimeter films from your childhood, you can be sure your children will enjoy seeing them. Your first bikini and the shock on your father's face, your senior prom, the bouffant hairdo, and the peace sign painted on your first car are images that may interest your kids. Also be sure to show any recent videos of your own kids.

Make a Movie: If you are fortunate enough to have your own video camera, make your own film as a family or group. You might make a monster film (using blow-up dinosaurs), a beach blanket surf film, or a takeoff on a television show, past or present.

Movie Night: If this movie production idea sounds too complicated or too time consuming, you can always take family members to the theater or drive-in to see a movie of their choice. Even simpler in this day and age is to rent a video movie and bring it home for viewing.

12 ▲ Nine to Five

The Idea: If you think your kids have no interest in what you do for a living, you're probably wrong. I suggest you bring your kids to your place of employment so that they can see what you do. You may choose to do this during the active working day or after closing hours when no one else is around.

Trading Places: Begin by taking your child to your office, factory, store, restaurant, church, or wherever else you may be employed. Ask your child to act out what he or she thinks you do on a typical day. If you are an executive, have your child sit at your desk. You play the secretary. If you are a secretary, have them play you, and you be the boss. If you work in a beauty salon, sit in one of the chairs and have them give you a shampoo.

The Tour: If you work in a small office or establishment, there may not be much to tour. However, if you work for a large company, a hospital, a factory, or some other large operation, give your children a tour of the organization. Let them see what you do every day. Give them a brief history of the company. Introduce them to your coworkers, your boss. Tell them about some of the equipment used.

The Equipment: I have memories of visiting the places where my parents worked when I was a kid. If you work in an office, don't think that it will be a complete bore for your child. Give him or her your adding machine for a while. Let your child type a letter on the word processor. Have him or her pretend to be chairman of the board and direct a meeting.

If you work on a construction site, under your supervision let your kids pound a hammer, cut a piece of wood, or put on a roof tile. If you work in a restaurant, let them turn on the mixer to make the pancake batter. If you are a doctor, explain to them some of the equipment you use.

Career Planning: Don't stop by giving your child a one-time tour of your work place. Together with some of your friends, take turns giving the dads, moms, and kids a tour of each other's work place. Not only will this be a time of fellowship and fun, it will help the kids start considering their career decisions early.

Once you have given your children a taste of what you do for a living, and what your neighbors or friends do, ask them what they would like to be when they grow up. If it is something different from what they have been exposed to already, try to arrange for them to see someone doing the job they mentioned.

13 ▲ It's a Free Country

The Idea: Take the kids away from their usual surroundings for a change. If you live in the heart of downtown, take them to the countryside. If you live out in the open, bring them to the nearest city. If you live in a suburb of a large city, you can do either.

For the City Dwellers: You can have a great deal of fun with your city-dwelling kids if you take them away from the buildings that are always around them. You can drive to a particular place in the country, or you may want to find as many types of terrain as possible in one day.

You can make the day educational by teaching your kids relevant geographic terms and locales. While touring the open spaces, try to make a special attempt to

> *Stop often to look at animals.* As you travel, stop to look at the horses, cows, birds, buffalo, seals, or other types of animals you may see along the way. If your children are

used to living in the city, they will probably enjoy seeing animals.

Walk in different terrain. Don't just drive from desert to meadow to shoreline to forest. As you approach a safe place to walk, stop the car and take a short hike, looking at plants, rocks, and scenery that may be new to your kids.

Take pictures. Be sure to bring a camera for you and one for the kids. Let them take pictures of the different things they see so that they can remember your day away.

For the Country Dwellers: If you live in the country, you probably do so because that's where you were raised or because you hate the big city. Even if the latter is true, your kids should form their own opinions about city life. Try to spend a day or two in a large city. Here are some ideas of activities for your excursion.

Visit a skyscraper. Take the kids to the top of the highest skyscraper in the city. If you're lucky, it will be a clear day, and they will get a view of the entire surroundings.

Visit historic spots. While you may be more interested in history than your kids, the big city near you may have relevance to what they're learning in school. It may contain a famous landmark of the Civil War, the house where an inventor lived, or the state capitol building.

Shop in an open-air market. In many big cities there are open-air markets that may be neglected by both country and city dwellers. If the city you visit has one of these large markets where people gather to buy fresh fruit, vegetables, and other goods, take the kids there, too.

Walk along the street. Sometime during your journey to the big city, go for a walk along the city streets. You will probably find a wide range of things to do and people to observe. This walk may generate some meaningful conversations about the ways of city life.

Whether you live in the city or in the country, try this exercise at least twice a year. It may help you and your kids recognize and appreciate the diversity of cultures and political freedoms we enjoy as Americans.

14 ▲ Lemon Aid

The Idea: Did you ever set up a lemonade stand when you were a child? If so, why not use your "expertise" and help your child or children set up their own stand in your front yard or at the nearest busy corner.

Starting a Business: Depending on how serious you are, and how much time you want to spend with your kids, I encourage you to teach them something about business while you are having fun setting up the stand. Develop a business plan.

> *Markup and pricing:* What is the cost of the goods used to make the lemonade? How much should a glass be sold for? Should we give a discount for three glasses to encourage multiple sales?

> *Finance:* Do we have coins in case people don't have the correct change? Do we need a loan from someone so we have enough change? What is our budget? What are our projected sales?

Marketing: What is the best location? Should we advertise? How large should our sign be? How do we get the word out?

Legal: Is there a city ordinance that prohibits us from doing this? Will they mind if we do this just one day? Do we need a business license?

Personnel: Who is scheduled to work the first shift? Who will make the goods and who will sell? Should we also sell cookies?

Operations: What resources do we need? Where can we find a table and two chairs?

Too complicated? Would you rather just turn the kids loose to tackle the world of high finances without a business plan? That's okay, too.

Other Options: Maybe "milking" a lemonade stand for all it's worth isn't your child's "cup of tea." If your children are resourceful, have them consider other ways to have fun and make a few cents at the same time.

Golf ball sales: I was on a golf course not long ago and saw two kids camped out at the tenth hole trying to sell the used golf balls they had found in the bushes. It seemed they had developed a marketing plan. Their sign read:

One golf ball	50 cents
Two golf balls	$1.00
Five golf balls	$2.00

A little advice: check with the pro shop first for permission.

Mowing: Remember the good old days when thirteen-year-old Scotty down the street mowed every lawn on the block? Does this still happen? Perhaps your child could re-generate an old tradition.

Pet-sitting: Maybe your child could start a business taking care of the neighbors' pets when they go away for long weekends or vacations.

House cleaning: In addition to doing chores around their own home to earn their allow-ance, some kids help others in the neigh-borhood to add even more to their piggy bank.

Ironing: Just the other day there was a story in the paper of a little girl who started ironing the family clothes for some extra money. She did such nice work that soon neighbors were bringing her their clothes to iron.

Make sure these ideas are pursued enthusiastically but lightly by your kids. They are too young to get caught up in the pressures of running a business.

15 ▲ Wanna Pet?

The Idea: This idea suggests that you find places right near your own home where you can take kids to see animals of different kinds. It further suggests some ways that you can make the world better for some of our four-legged friends.

Down on the Farm: If you live in the country this may be an easy excursion for you. If you live in the city, you may have to plan ahead for a trip to the farm. In either case, your child will probably have no problem finding things to look at once you're there. Here are a couple of ideas you may want to consider, although the owner of the farm may be able to give you more suggestions.

> *Baby animals:* Try to find as many baby animals as you can. One of the most amusing sights for children of all ages is that of a mother pig and her baby piglets. Look also for baby calves, ponies, sheep and goats. Some farms also have bunnies and chicks.

> *Feeding:* See if you can be a part of feeding time. If your children are small, you may

want to let them throw feed to the chickens. If they are older, they may be able to feed some of the larger animals.

Ride the tractor: If the farm is one where crops are grown, your children will no doubt get a thrill out of riding in a tractor or watching the process involved in sowing or harvesting crops. Show them how corn is picked, how the irrigation channels function, and where grain is stored.

County Fair: If a visit to a farm is too difficult for your part of the country, consider going to the next county fair. Even in the middle of the Los Angeles metropolitan area, local county fairs are always well-stocked with baby piglets, prize cattle, and other farm animals.

A Call to the Wild: I suggest you take the kids to "see the buffalo roam." There are parts of our country where the buffalo do still roam. If there are none near you, perhaps you can take the kids on a drive to a place where you know there are deer. Children don't need to see only large and magnificent animals. For most, a squirrel or chipmunk will do. Ask your child what his or her favorite animal is. Then do whatever you can to observe one in the wild. If the answer is a bunny, your task may be simple. If it is a rhinoceros, you may have a long way to go!

A Trip to the Pound: Visit the local animal shelter or pound frequently with your kids. Perhaps your kids will want to face the challenge of finding homes for as many of the animals as possible. The next time you go to your local animal shelter, take along a camera that produces instant photos. As you photograph each of your favorite animals, write their names on the bottom of the picture. Then, as you are leaving the shelter, find out the procedure for adopting an animal. The kids can then show pictures of pets needing homes to neighbors and friends. Have them start with just one or two animals. If they take on too many more than that, they may become discouraged. Once they do find someone willing to take one of the pets, they will have the satisfaction of knowing they helped out a lonely animal.

16 ▲ Driver's Ed

The Idea: On those longer trips play word games to pass the time and have fun. This suggestion could be entertaining for kids of all ages—even those over fifty!

Games to Ponder: You may remember games that you played in the car with your family or friends as you were growing up. But in case you don't remember any, or in case you have never played car games, we have listed a few below for you to consider.

> *Find the fifty states:* This can be an ongoing game that you play with your family, or it can be a game you use during a long trip, perhaps across country. You may want to begin this game every calendar year, when every player starts with a clean slate on January first.
>
> The goal of this game is to find a license plate for all fifty of the United States. You may want to make up a form for everyone listing all fifty states (and the District of Columbia). Then as players see each state's

license on passing or parked cars, they
mark it down on the form by stating the
date and location where the plate was seen.
The first person to see the plate gets the
credit. Or you can play as a team, using one
form for the entire family.

Travel bingo: In this game everyone has a
card similar to one you would have when
playing bingo (five squares across and five
squares down). Instead of having letters
and numbers in each square, you draw a
picture or print the name of different things
you might see from your car (for example,
cows, boats, detour signs, or a stalled car).
(You might be able to find ready-made
travel bingo cards in a toy store.) Each time
you see one of the objects shown on your
card, you mark it off. Once you've found
everything in one horizontal, vertical, or di-
agonal line, you win that round of the game.

Find the landmark: A fun game to play with
smaller children is to have them all look for
a specific landmark. When I was a child our
family would play a game on the way to Disneyland. The first one to see the Matterhorn mountain "won." Instead of a specific
landmark like the Matterhorn, you might
want to have everyone search for the first
star at dusk, or for a particular brand of gas
station (especially if you're low on fuel).

Name the object: In this game someone thinks of a particular item somewhere in the world. It can be as near as the steering wheel of your car or as silly as the left ear of the Statue of Liberty. The other people in the car have to guess what the object is based on asking questions that can be answered with a "yes" or "no." For example, if the object is the Eiffel Tower, someone could start with the question: "Is it located in the United States?" From there, others might narrow it down to the proper continent, country, and city. By then, it's a matter of naming various landmarks.

A trip to the market: Another game you can play is one that requires lots of concentration. The first person starts with the sentence, "When I went to the market I bought . . ." Then he or she names something that starts with the letter A. (It doesn't have to be something you could actually buy at a market. It could be something silly.)

So, the first person might say, "When I went to the market I bought an anteater." The second person must repeat the first person's item and then add an item that starts with the letter B.

The second person might say, "When I went to the market I bought an anteater and a bathing suit." The third person must then

name those two items plus one that starts
with the letter C. Once everyone has had a
turn, go back to the first person and continue with the next letter.

17 ▲ A World of Fun

The Idea: If you or your child find geography a bore, maybe you need to try learning methods that might make it fun. These ideas allow you to learn more about our country and our world, while at the same time to have fun and provide a learning experience for your child.

Supplies: You will need to find the largest possible world map you can. You may also want to find an equally large map of the United States, since much of your study may be about our own country. You should also get many pushpins in a variety of colors. Or, you may want to get some pins that have tiny flags of different colors. If you don't want pin holes on your walls, you can purchase a corkboard large enough to go behind your map.

Setting Up Your Guidelines: As soon as you get your map, you and your kids should set guidelines for using the map. Answers to the following questions can be used to make these guidelines.

- How often are you going to add another item to the map?
- Can you commit to adding one new pin a day?
- How much time will you spend on this project each week, discussing the significance of each pin?
- What system are you going to use for the colored pins?

  For example, red pins might represent significant places for our family members (birthplaces, grandparents' homes); blue pins could be state or country capitals; and green pins could be places where current news events are taking place.
- Do you want to keep a journal recording each city or area you mark?

Using Your World Map: Once you have purchased your map and pins and have established your guidelines, begin learning and sharing geography with one another. You may want to begin by marking the following locations on your maps.

Birthplace of each member of your family
Hometowns of relatives
Places the family traveled to on vacation
Cities you've traveled to on business
Capital cities of our states and of countries
   around the world
Location of events currently in the news

How many families actually talk about current events? You may find that your kids were not interested in the news until you started the map project. After setting up the map you can say, "Right now our president is in Venezuela. Do you know where that is?" Or, "Today the Super Bowl was played in Miami. Can you find Miami on the map?" Or, "Our church supports a family in Vanuatu. Does anyone know where Vanuatu is?"

Living Room Map: Another geography learning exercise is to pretend that your living room is a map of the United States. "That corner of the room is Maine, this one Florida . . ." Ask your child to stand where he thinks Texas should be located. Or ask him or her where Grandma and Grandpa would live. You'll have fun, and they will increase their knowledge of various place names and approximate locations.

18 ▲ On the Right Track

The Idea: Kids love trains of all shapes and sizes. Here are some ideas of how you can better "train" your children.

All Aboard: Perhaps the most fun you can have with trains is to take your kids for a ride on a real train. Here are some ideas to consider based upon the age of your child.

> *Park train:* In many cities there are small trains for children at local public parks or at smaller amusement parks. Perhaps there is a carnival in town that has a small train ride.

> *Zoo train:* Go to the zoo and find out if it has a train ride. Then you can visit the zoo *and* ride the train.

> *Passenger train:* For kids too big to enjoy the park or zoo train, consider taking them on a short trip on a passenger train. You don't have to spend a weekend or even a night away. Simply buy tickets for some nearby location, and spend the day picnicking or

visiting a tourist attraction. Then take the train home. This is a fun way to spend a day with your child. He or she will be much more excited taking the train than the car.

Cable cars: Of course, the city most famous for its cable cars is San Francisco. If you visit this city, be sure to take the kids on a cable car ride. Or perhaps you know of someplace near you that offers the same pleasurable event.

The Next Best Thing: If you cannot take the kids on a train ride, or even if you do, here are some other ideas to keep them on the right track.

Train museum: While climbing aboard an old train is nowhere near as exciting as taking an actual ride, you can consider a visit to a train museum near you. Some train museums feature old steam locomotives and other old cars, while others feature room after room of model trains for kids of all ages to enjoy.

Model train: No kid should go through childhood without a model train, especially at Christmas time. While some sets are expensive, you can do things to save money. For example, consider making your own "terrain" for your train to travel on. Get a large piece of plywood, paint it green, and use sand, gravel, and moss to create a country-side setting. Create small buildings using popsicle sticks. You can even buy or make little people to inhabit the towns where your train will travel.

Tell stories and sing songs: I couldn't include a chapter on trains without mentioning the old story about the little train that could. Many adults remember that story as they face the "uphill" challenges of life. They might even be heard to say, "I think I can. I think I can . . ." Tell this story to your kids. You might also sing the old favorite song, "I've Been Working on the Railroad," with your kids. And don't forget kid-sized blue striped overalls for die-hard train fans.

Try some of these suggestions with your little engineers. You will have lots of fun . . . "all the live-long day."

19 ▲ Zoo Who?

The Idea: Take the kids to the zoo. Talk about a simple idea! Even if you've gone once or twice over the last few years, very few kids will ever get tired of visiting the animals. Children of all ages find the zoo a fun place to go. It might even bring out more of the kid in you!

Enroute to the Zoo: While driving or riding to the zoo, have everyone in the car try to think of songs that have animals in them. Then together, sing those songs. Make a list of how many animals you have named. Try to find in the zoo each of the animals you've listed. Here are a few songs that mention animals—just to get you started.

"Mary Had A Little Lamb"
"Old McDonald Had A Farm"
"Animal Crackers in My Soup"
"Three Little Fishes"

Once Inside the Zoo: Here are some ideas to make your day at the zoo even more memorable. You may want to try them all or just pick one or two.

Have a photo contest.   Give everyone in the family one of those new cameras you use once and then take in for developing. Conduct your own photo contest. Set a time when you will all get together to award the prize for the best animal photo.

Ride the elephant.   If the zoo has an elephant ride, don't just put your kids on. Ride with them!

Imitate the animals.   As you watch new animals, see who in the family can best imitate them. For example, if you see an ostrich, take turns walking like an ostrich. If you watch the seals, take turns barking back at them.

Feed the animals.   Often there are animals the zoo will let you feed. Try not to miss this opportunity. Offer a peanut to the elephant. Throw a fish to the seal. Let the llama eat pellets from your hand.

Adopt an Animal.   Some city zoos have programs where patrons can make a contribution and become sponsors for a certain animal. Adopt an animal for your child. Each time you visit the local zoo, you can make it a habit to visit the new member of the family.

20 ▲ Tour de City

The Idea: You don't have to go very far to have an adventure with your kids. Simply find some activities to do right in your own hometown.

Gather Some History: If you've lived all your life in the city where your kids are growing up, you probably know quite a bit of its history. You'll be able to say things like, "Right where this shopping center stands is where my high school auditorium once stood. Over there behind that gas station was the biggest roller coaster in the state."

If you are not originally from the city where you now live, see if there is a local historical society holding meetings. If not, try to interview someone who knows the history of the city and the surrounding area. Meet with him or her and hear a few stories prior to taking the kids on your private journey.

Visit the City Facilities: While your child may be bored hearing the complete history of your city, there are certain things in the city he or she might like to see.

Fire station: Almost every child loves a fire truck, and most kids look up to firefighters. Try calling to see if you can arrange a tour of your local fire station for your kids. Many fire chiefs will cooperate and gladly give you a tour. They might also tell you of an upcoming open house.

Police station: Try the same thing with the police department. An officer may take the time to show you the jail cells, explain a case one of the detectives is investigating, or let you go for a ride in a patrol car.

City hall: Depending on the size of your city, you might be able to arrange a tour of your city hall and meet your mayor.

Other Landmarks:

Take the kids to historical areas that might interest them. Again, depending on the length of time you have lived there, the stories concerning these attractions may fascinate them. You might also

- Show them the oldest building in town.
- Show them places important in your past.
- Show them places like the hospital where they were born.
- Take them to places with historical significance concerning the city's founders or early immigrants.

21 ▲ The Joy of Giving

The Idea: This way of having fun with your kids is designed to bring some joy into the lives of others also. Here are ways to bring a little sunshine into the lives of less fortunate kids or adults.

Ways of Sharing Your Heart: I could write another book on ways to help the poor, lonely, or sick. For now, let me suggest ways you and your kids can help other children.

> *Sponsor a foreign child:* There are a number of organizations, such as World Vision or Compassion International, that allow you to sponsor a child in a poor country. You and your child could sponsor such a child together.
>
> As part of most sponsorship programs, you are able to correspond with the sponsored child. Help your child write letters, paint pictures to send, and study the culture of your sponsored child.
>
> *Christmas shopping:* Every kid loves a toy store. This year, as you prepare for Christ-

mas, have your child pick out a very special toy for some other child. You can donate the toy to organizations like Toys for Tots or the Angel Tree project of Prison Fellowship, which provides toys for children of prison inmates. There are also programs to provide toys for children that are in the hospital over the Christmas holidays.

Adopt a family: Perhaps you know of a family or elderly person in your area that needs help with grocery shopping or some chore around the house. Encourage your children to help.

Even if the people needing assistance are from a different culture, and communication is awkward at first, your child may develop very special friendships. You may be surprised at how much fun two kids from different cultures can have with one another, if they are placed in the right setting. If they are young enough, they probably have not developed the biases we tend to develop as we get older.

Forgotten children: Ask your child if there is someone at school who doesn't seem to fit in because of being different in some way. Ask your child if he or she would like to invite that child over some day. You may learn something about the joy that comes from reaching out to someone who feels alone in the world.

Pediatric ward: If you really want to make a change in some child's life, take your kids to visit the pediatric ward in the local hospital. Some seriously ill children long to have other children come in and play cards or other games with them. Check with your local children's hospital to see if there are children that you and your child could visit. You may be the "medicine" they need to encourage them back to health.

Adopt a grandparent: Perhaps your child's grandparents live far away. But even if they live next door, your child can benefit from bringing joy and companionship to a lonely person living in a retirement home. See if you can find an elderly person that your child can adopt as a grandma or grandpa. Such a relationship may enrich and prolong life.

If your child is willing to participate in any of these activities, you have a very special child. Even though these suggestions may lack the "fun" of the others mentioned in this book, we hope you will consider them. Children who experience the joy of reaching out to help people in need will better understand what "family" and "fun" can truly mean.

22 ▲ Role Reversal

The Idea: Implementing this idea will be a learning experience for all involved. Parents become the kids for the day (or evening), and your children become the parents.

Setting Up the Plan: A few days before you decide to begin, talk the idea over with your kids. You might say something like this: "We're going to try something new Saturday. From the time we get up in the morning until the time we go to bed, you are going to pretend you're the parents, and we're going to pretend we're the kids."

If you're not quite brave enough for a full day, try it for an evening during the week and set a time of day such as 5 p.m. for the reversal to begin. You might want to review the following ideas with your kids, so they, too, can plan for the day. You will have the most fun if you don't share each other's plans.

Some Ideas for the Parents (Played by the Kids): You probably have many years left before you will be parents. It might look easy, but this is your chance to find out what your parents deal with on a daily basis. Consider these ideas as you plan your day.

Morning: Before the "kids" begin their day, you will need to make sure they are properly fed. Cereal and toast will usually do the trick for a Saturday morning. Once breakfast is served, ask the kids if they have fed the pets and finished their Saturday chores. (This is your chance to have them mow the lawn, take out the garbage, or clean their room!)

Afternoon: If your parents normally make you lunch on Saturday, then you should make their lunch today. If everyone is usually on their own, then stick to that routine. Surprise your "kids" after lunch with some sort of excursion nearby the house, such as a walk to the playground or a trip to the ice skating rink.

Evening: Take your "kids" out to their favorite restaurant for dinner. (You may want to have your parents give you money the day before to cover "your" dinner treat.) After dinner, perhaps a drive-in movie will be in store. Once you get there, put the "kids" in the back seat. That night as you put them to bed, be sure to read a bedtime story and encourage them to say their prayers.

Some Ideas for the Kids (Played by the Parents):
Remember the old days when you were kids? The days when your biggest problem was to decide what show to watch on Saturday morning or which game to play with friends? Well, now you can return to those days of tough decisions. Consider these ideas as you plan your day.

Morning: If your kids typically wake you on the one morning you like to sleep in, remember that you're switching the roles today. Set your alarm for 5:00 a.m. and visit your "parents" bedroom. Tell them it's time to get up.

Afternoon: Remember, you are the kids. That might mean you sit around all morning and afternoon in front of the television. If your "parents" didn't plan anything, that means you're free to do what you want.

Evening: Since it is Saturday night, your "parents" might treat you to dinner and to a fun activity. If you want to stay up late, fuss with them as soon as they say it's time for bed. Thank them at the end of the day for being such wonderful parents.

When the role reversal has ended, be sure to assume your old identity. (You may like being who you've been for the last few hours.) Sit as a group and talk about the fun you had in your role reversal.

23 ▲ Three Rings

The Idea: Go to the circus!

Preparing for the Day: This event will take some planning because you will need to find out when a circus is coming to your city or a city near you. Start by calling the convention center, arena, or other locations where the circus would typically perform. If you come up empty-handed, check your paper regularly for news of such an event.

Once you find out the date, start the event off right. Don't merely tell the children you're taking them to the circus, make a fun and special invitation for them. Perhaps a bouquet of balloons with a card attached, which says, "The circus is coming to town on January 31. And you're invited!" Or, you may want to create a circus scene in their bedroom using a menagerie of miniature animals. Next to the display place a card inviting them to the big top. Or, why not dress up like a clown and invite them in person?

If you are creative with a needle and thread, create a skirt for your daughter or a sweatshirt for your son with various circus animals cut out of felt and sewn to the fabric. You might decorate the animals with glitter or sequins.

Previewing the Show: While you will probably not be able to preview the circus, you can rent one of the great old circus movies. This will get the kids excited for the real thing.

If you live in a place where the circus raises a big tent rather than performing indoors, find out what day the circus workers will be setting up. See if they will allow you to bring your kids and watch the tent being assembled.

During the Circus: Watch your kids faces as the circus unfolds. If there are three rings operating at once, be sure to point out anything they might be missing. See if the management gives the public an opportunity to get a closer look at the lions, tigers, and elephants. Maybe you'll get lucky and one of the circus employees will give you a special tour. It never hurts to ask.

After the Circus: On your way home, ask the kids what they most enjoyed about the day. If they could be anyone in the circus, who would it be? Why?

When you get home, continue the fun. Dress up the family dog like the dogs were dressed at the circus. Write and illustrate a story about your day at the big top to share with friends and family who weren't along.

24 ▲ Root, Root, Root for the Home Team

The Idea: How much more American can you get than a baseball (Dodger) game? (Parenthesis put in by the author, who happens to be biased by Dodger Blue.) Grab the kids and go to a ball game. Whatever team you root for, it needs you and the kids there.

Even if you don't live near a city with a professional baseball, football, or basketball team, you can attend a game at the local university or high school.

Getting Ready to Go: Before you get in the car, be sure you have the right equipment: a glove to catch the foul balls, the binoculars, and, of course, a baseball cap displaying your team's emblem or colors.

On the way to the game you may want to warm up for the seventh inning stretch by singing "Take Me Out to the Ball Game" two or three times. If you are attending a college game of some kind, you may want to record their fight song on a tape so that you can play it on the way. If all else fails, tape

the theme song from *Rocky.* That will get you moti-
vated to do just about anything.

Pregame Activities: I recommend that you
get to the game early to avoid the traffic. Sit down
and enjoy your hot dog and peanuts before the
crowds get there. Watch the excitement build as
people enter the stadium or arena.

If you're bored, buy a program and play a game of
puns while waiting for the first pitch.
   Simply make a riddle or pun out of the players'
names. The person giving the answer must use a
player's first and last name, but not necessarily in
the proper order. Here are a few examples using
men who used to play for my favorite team.

> *Example One:*   What did the mechanic say to
> one Dodger as he got in his car after the
> repairs were complete?
>
> Answer: Start your Mota, Manny. (Player:
> Manny Mota)
>
> *Example Two:*   What did the headlines on the
> sports page say when one of the Dodgers
> ran off and got married unexpectedly?
>
> Answer: Dave Elopes. (Player: Davey
> Lopes)

Example Three: What did the police detective say to a Dodger who rambled while being questioned about a crime?

Answer: Just the Koufax, Sandy, just the Koufax. (Player: Sandy Koufax)

Watching the Game: During the game, explain to your kids what is going on. Be more interested in their questions and comments than in the outcome of the game. Yell a lot. Laugh a lot.

Going Home: Before you leave the stadium or arena, buy your kids a souvenir. It will mean a lot to them.

25 ▲ For Shore

The Idea: Spend a day at the beach. Whether it is the shoreline of a lake near your home or the sands of the great wide ocean, there are many waterside activities you can do to have fun with the children in your life.

What to Bring: Bring whatever you will need to be comfortable and whatever the kids will need to have fun. Here are a few essentials I suggest and some space for you to complete the list of items to bring.

- Sunscreen and/or suntan lotion
- Blankets or towels
- Beach chairs
- Reading material
- Picnic basket and ice chest
- Shovels and buckets
- Rafts or body boards
- Hats or visors
- Frisbee or football

_____
_____
_____

What to Do: There are lots of things kids can do at the beach. A few of them are listed for you below.

> *Sand castles:*   What is a day at the beach without a sand castle? Everyone seems to have his own building technique. Some people use nothing but their bare hands to mold and shape their work of art. Others fill buckets with wet sand and then turn the buckets upside down to create towers. Still others use the drip method. By taking very wet sand and letting it drip from your finger tips, you can form spires for the castle. Then there are people who not only create a moat around the castle but creatively construct a drawbridge from pieces of driftwood. With these methods in mind, you and the kids can consider having a sand-castle-making contest.

> *Bury someone's feet:*   Simply dig a hole. Have someone sit on the edge and dangle his feet in the hole. Fill in the rest of the hole with sand. Have him stand up. Suddenly the person will be a foot shorter—maybe even two feet! When you're done, be careful not to get distracted and walk away. He may never get out!

> *Skip rocks:*   If your shoreline day is at a lake where the water is flat and glassy, practice

your rock-skipping techniques. See who can set the record for the most skips.

Swim: Whether your day is at the lake or in the ocean, take the kids out for a swim. Bring along rafts, if you are on a lake; or body boards to ride the waves, if you are at the beach.

Tide pools: If you are at the beach, do whatever you can to find the best tide pools. I've yet to find a child that is not amazed at the hundreds of little creatures that live among the rocks. Hermit crabs, sea urchins, and tiny fish are all part of God's special playground.

Look for shells or rocks: At the beach, wander around the shoreline and search for sea shells. Even if you are at a lake, there may be pretty rocks or pieces of driftwood worth collecting.

End your day at the shore by sitting quietly and watching the sun set. Discuss why each sunset is different from every other one.

26 ▲ Star Light, Star Bright

The Idea: Stars are fascinating. They're above us every night as we sleep, yet we so often take their beauty for granted. I recommend you spend some time learning about the stars with your kids.

Star Gazing: Here are some ways you can experience the cosmos with your kids.

Planetarium or observatory: Find out where the closest planetarium or observatory is to your home. Inquire with your local park service, library, or any university located in your area, if you are having trouble finding one near you. Plan a day or evening to visit. Each observatory's displays and activities will vary. Most will have educational displays, which will teach you about constellations. Some will have a high-powered telescope, which you and the kids can look through to view the planets and stars.

Telescope: While you will never be able to afford a telescope quite like the ones used in major observatories, you can purchase or borrow a telescope and spend time viewing the moon and stars on your own. Even store-bought telescopes allow you to see the craters on the moon and focus directly on other planets in the solar system.

Eclipse: Next time there is a solar or lunar eclipse in your area, read about the event. Try to explain this phenomenon to your kids or simulate what will happen using tennis balls and flashlights, or other objects around the house. As the eclipse approaches, teach your kids to use special viewing procedures, since the sun can cause permanent eye damage.

Camping trip: Shortly after your time in the planetarium, or after you have spent time teaching your kids about the various constellations, plan a camping trip far away from the city lights so that the stars will be their brightest. Even if you prefer to use a tent, begin your night by lying under the stars. If wilderness camping is not your thing, find a place away from the city lights near your house and spend an evening looking at the stars.

You may see what looks like a star moving across the sky. If it is too high to be an airplane, it may well be a satellite circling our planet. Talk about what you see.

27 ▲ Bike and Tyke

The Idea: Spend time exercising with your kids. You'll be spending some fun time together and getting healthier, too.

Some Suggestions: Perhaps you already exercise regularly on your own. As your kids get old enough, include them in your workout routines. Here are some ideas.

Jogging: There seem to be more people jogging these days than ever before. Even if you are a marathon runner, surely you can allow your kids to jog around the block a few times with you as you warm up. Or, you may let them run the entire distance, if you run shorter courses.

Aerobics: This form of exercise is so good for you, and a good workout can be fun! If you belong to a gym, or if you regularly do aerobics at home in front of your television, have the kids join you from time to time.

Biking: This is perhaps my favorite suggestion for adults and children exercising together. If you are lucky enough to live near a well-maintained and safe bike path along a scenic route be sure to use it. Or, perhaps you can ride around your neighborhood. Make a surprise visit to a friend or relative a few blocks away by riding there with the kids. Wherever you go, be sure the kids know the basics of safe riding.

Walking or hiking: In almost every part of the country there are hiking trails to investigate. Call your local park service or the National Park Service to find out about new places you could explore.
Plan a day with the kids when you can make a lunch, grab a small backpack, and go on a journey for a few hours. Consider nearby mountain trails, or hike through a part of the desert. Maybe you live near the beach and can walk along the water into some coves. If all else fails, grab the family and go for a walk around your neighborhood.

Swim: If your community has an exercise pool, and your child knows how to swim, take him or her to the pool and swim a few laps.

28 ▲ Fun for Sail

The Idea: Take the kids out for a day of sailing, rowing, or floating on the water. If you don't want to go out on a boat, there are still many things you can do in a harbor or marina setting.

Board Your Vessel: There is a wide variety of activities you can do with your kids on a boat. First, you must decide if you prefer power or sail. Here are possible boating scenarios you can consider regardless of your preference.

> *Amusement park:* If your child is little, he or she will be perfectly satisfied boating in the kiddie ride at the local carnival or amusement park. The kids sit in tub-sized boats and go around in circles, while all the proud parents wave and fumble with their cameras.

> *Rowboat:* The simplest way for you to join your kids on a boat ride may be to rent a rowboat and take them out on a nearby lake. Perhaps you can teach them how to

row as part of the experience. If you don't want to work quite as hard, you might be able to rent a boat with an outboard motor.

Sailboat: If you are an experienced sailor, you may want to rent a small sailboat (fourteen foot or so) and take the kids for a spin around the lake or marina.

Whale watch: If you live near the ocean or plan to visit there soon, you and your kids may enjoy a guided whale watch excursion. You may see the spout and topside of one of these large creatures. If you're lucky, you may see whales jump twenty feet into the air, a sight everyone should see at least once in a lifetime.

Paddle boat: Many city parks or amusement parks have small paddle boats, which you power with your legs much like a bicycle. If your kids can reach the pedals, let them get a workout.

Ferryboat: With this boating option, you never have to get out of your car! Find out where the nearest ferryboat is located, and take it wherever it is bound. If your kids have never seen a ferryboat, they will be particularly amazed when you drive your car aboard.

Water-ski: If your kids are the more athletic type, take them water-skiing. To take part in this activity, however, you will probably have to know someone who has a ski boat.

If You Lack Sea Legs: Even if you don't enjoy boating, you can still allow your kids to get exposure to the boating world. Here are a few ideas.

Locks: Take your kids to one of the locks along the old Erie Canal or any others in America. Your child may see a ship enter the water at one level and drop dozens of feet as water is let out of the lock. The ship then continues on its journey, safely avoiding dangerous rapids or other hazards.

Naval yard: Visit the large ships that make up our U.S. Navy. On special occasions you and your child may be allowed to enter a submarine, aircraft carrier, or battleship.

Boat shows: Even if you never have the intention of buying a boat, visit a boat show next time it comes to town or a town near you. At the major boat shows you can see everything from rowboats to extravagant yachts.

Regattas: During the bicentennial of our country there was a tour of tall ships that went up and down both coasts. A similar event took place in 1992, celebrating the five hundredth anniversary of Columbus' voyage. If your child is a boat lover, seeing this type of flotilla would be an unforgettable experience.

29 ▲ What's Buggin' You?

The Idea: If you have a fear of insects, you may not want to attempt this suggestion. But if insects don't bug you, the kids will greatly enjoy spending time with you as they explore the incredible world of insects.

Equipment Needed: The amount of equipment you'll need depends upon how seriously you plan to study insects and their way of life. If you just want to go out and look for bugs, a simple shoe box will do. If your child seems interested enough to start a new hobby, you may want to purchase a book that explains the different types of insects. Or, the kids may want to begin a butterfly collection, which requires special display cases and nets.

What's Bugging You: Think back to your own childhood. Were there insects that you found particularly fascinating? Here are some ideas about how activities with insects can become memorable for your children.

> *Fireflies:* Perhaps the most fascinating insect for children is the firefly. We miss out on

these insects in southern California, but other people throughout the country get to see these bright little stars dance in their gardens during warm summer nights. Your child may want to get a jar with a screen over the top and collect a firefly or two for a few hours. I recommend releasing them so they can live to dance in someone else's garden.

Honey bees: A local beekeeper might be willing to show you and your kids a working hive. With the right equipment, such as netting and gloves, the study of a hive can be a safe and instructional activity. You might also enjoy the taste of honey still in the comb!

Caterpillars: Perhaps you have an old fish aquarium not in use. If so, put a screen over the top of the aquarium and place a couple of caterpillars inside. Make sure you give the caterpillars plenty of different types of leaves, including leaves from the tree or plant where you found them. You might be able to see the caterpillar form a cocoon. Better yet, find an existing cocoon for your aquarium, carefully cutting off the twig on which it is formed. Once the new moth or butterfly has emerged, set it free in your backyard.

Ants: No kid should go through childhood
without experiencing the wonder of an ant
farm. Many toy stores or hobby shops will
have ant farm kits, including instructions on
how to build and maintain your insect community. Help your child gather the right
materials, and observe the ant colony each
day as the hard-working critters build their
little city.

Even if you don't get an ant farm, try finding an ant hill to explore. See if you can find
ants that are carrying a morsel of food several times their weight. Discuss this with
your child and see where your conversation
leads. ("Have you ever felt like something
was on your mind that was too big for you
to handle alone?")

Remember roley-poley or pill bugs, and those ugly
potato bugs? Remember watching a spider build a
web? Can you think of any more memories about
crawling creatures? Share them with your kids.

30 ▲ How Now Dow Jones

The Idea: Whether you've become a good investor or not, help your kids achieve their own financial goals. Teach them ways to invest their resources while they are still young.

The Young Investor: You may be thinking that this suggestion is for people who have a lot of money. Quite the contrary is true. You can teach your children about investments regardless of your net worth. Just think, if your children could learn from your mistakes, they might be more financially secure than you when they are your age. Here are ways you can teach your kids how to be little investors.

> *Stock market:* Do you think the stock market sounds like a bore for children? Maybe for some. But others will take great interest in lessons about how stocks are bought and sold. I remember my dad taking my two brothers and me to the local stock exchange to see all the excitement.
>
> While we were there, he asked, "If you

could pick any company to invest in, what would it be?" Loving airplanes, I picked American Airlines, one brother picked Walt Disney Enterprises, and the other picked what is now a thriving fast-food restaurant chain. Can you imagine where my dad would be if he had invested money in these stocks?

Even if you do not have any money to invest, pretend that you have a bank account and have each member of the family pick a few stocks, each person investing equal amounts. Keep track of how each person's "portfolio" is doing over a period of time. This can become a very fun game for the serious, investment-curious child.

Savings account: Teach your child how to deposit a portion of his or her money for safe keeping and to earn interest. Perhaps a part of each week's allowance can go to the savings account. One savings account might be a place the kids can keep money to be used for entertainment, gifts, and other expenses. Another account could be opened as a lifelong savings fund. This account could have restrictions, such as withdrawal only in emergencies or for the cost of college tuition.

Real estate: Your children investing in real estate? Probably not. Many adults cannot afford to purchase their own home. But like the stock market example previously mentioned, consider teaching your children about real estate investments by using imaginary money.

You might show them that they can purchase a home with their make-believe 125,000 dollars. Or, they can purchase a four-unit apartment building. Look in the paper to see if you can find some homes or apartments for this amount. (In areas like the one I live in, you will probably need at least 250,000 dollars in imaginary money to buy a house or apartment building.)

Then track the example real estate investments over time. What is the difference in income taxes if you rent a home versus purchasing a home? Is it smarter to buy a home for which you will make payments? Or is it wiser to buy an apartment building that will yield rental income? Keep your game going for a couple of years, then go back and find out whether your sample house has gone up in value. Would it have been a good investment? Is saving for a home worth the effort?

You can also teach your kids about investing in property by showing them how you take care of possessions. Be sure they know that a car or home kept in good condition can become a very valuable investment. Perhaps when they understand this idea they will be less likely to take the family car and house for granted.

31 ▲ Runway Runaway

The Idea: Go to the nearest commercial airport and find a safe spot as close as you can to either end of the runway. Depending on the airport, you may be able to get closer to the planes on the end of the runway where they take off. In other cases, you may get closer to the area of the airport where the planes land.

While You're Watching: You will probably have lots of things to talk about with your kids as you watch the planes take off and land above you. The following suggestions for activities may bring some added enjoyment to your time together.

Name the airline: As a jet approaches see which member of the family can name its airline first. After your first trip, you may find your kids studying airline logos in preparation for future visits. Keep a running tally of who has the best record of recognizing the various airlines.

Guess the destination: Just for fun, have each person guess what city is the final destination of a particular jet. No one will be able to tell if their guesses were correct. However, if you want to get serious, buy an airline guide. And, assuming the planes are on schedule, you can look up the destination of each departing flight.

Name the type of aircraft: You will probably want to play this game if either you or one of your children are flying enthusiasts. See if anyone can name the type of aircraft taking off or landing. Is it a Boeing 767, an L-1011, or a Super 80?

Other games you can play: Make up your own games as you spend a few hours near the runway. Or, see if you can answer these questions.

- How many tires are on a Boeing 747?
- How many engines are on a DC-10?
- How do airplanes fly?
- What colors are the lights on each end of the wings?

Other Airport Options: If you and your kids get tired of watching jets take off and land, here are a couple of other ways you can have fun at the airport.

Go to an air show: Call your local military base or municipal airport to see if an air show is coming to your area. If so, mark the date on the family calendar and plan to attend. Such shows are usually quite spectacular.

Tour the control tower: Many airports will allow the public to tour the control tower, if you arrange for it in advance, especially if you mention that you want to teach your children about airport management. You may decide to wait until the airport has an open house day.

Go flying!   Perhaps you or your kids have never been up in a small plane before. If you have a friend who is a pilot, ask if you and the kids can arrange a short flight. Or, if it is within your budget, you can charter a plane at your local airport. Ask the pilot if he or she will take you over special places such as your home or the kids' school.

32 ▲ You Auto Know

The Idea: Whether your children are toddlers or teenagers, I can almost guarantee that they are interested in cars. Based on their age, your budget, and their physical abilities, you can share this excitement with them.

For the Toddler: If your child is a toddler, here are a few suggestions for fun with cars.

> *Car seat driver:* Most toddlers reach an age when they like to imitate mom, dad, an aunt or uncle, or any other respected adult. Often driving a car is one of the earliest copied behaviors. There are a number of toys on the market that allow your child to pretend he or she is driving. While safely in a car seat, your child can have his or her own toy steering wheel, horn, and turn signal.

> *Living room driver:* There are also a number of toys on the market that are safe for indoor driving. That is, as long as your furniture is childproof or broken-in by older children. These toys are small plastic cars,

propelled by foot power, and complete with a driver's door, steering wheel, and trunk.

Amusement park driver: In most amusement parks there are rides designed for small toddlers or preschool kids. Your auto enthusiasts will love sitting in one of those cars that go around and around. They will get such delight thinking they are the ones who are steering it in endless circles. Notice how they imitate your driving actions as they take a turn behind the wheel.

For the Elementary Age Child: As your kids get older they will no longer be interested in plastic auto imitations. They will be more interested in the real thing. Something with speed. Yet, they won't be quite old enough to drive. Consider one of these options.

Game room track: Your middle-school-aged kids might enjoy having their own race track in their bedroom or the family room. There are some sets that operate by electricity similar to a train set, and some that are wound up, and others that operate simply by gravity.

Remote control cars: While most people may not be able to afford them, kids are fascinated by the modern remote control cars that are on the market. Recent technology has greatly improved these toys, which are able to simulate the maneuvers of full-sized vehicles.

Bumper cars: The carnival ride mentioned above will be far too juvenile for your preteen and early teen-aged kids. They're ready for bumper cars. While these rides are not found in as many places as they were twenty years ago, you can still find them in some carnivals and amusement parks.

Go-carts: These little cars have come a very long way since we were children. They now have tracks that simulate the larger professional tracks and provide hours of fun for older children and adults alike.

Auto race: Many kids, regardless of their age, will enjoy seeing an auto race. Whether you see a demolition derby, dragsters, a stock car race, or the Indianapolis 500, your child is sure to have fun with part or all of the festivities.

For the Adolescents: There is usually only one thing that will excite teenagers of driving age: getting the keys to the family car. Even though your child may be taking drivers education courses at school, perhaps you can take him or her to a large empty parking lot and allow him or her a turn at the wheel. Of course, the only thing more exciting than driving the family car is having a car of one's own.

33 ▲ Call Collect

The Idea: Help your child or children start a collection of some kind. Maybe they have already started collecting something, and you can help them further their hobby.

Collectibles: The variety of things your child can collect are almost infinite. Some of the collectible items are more obvious. Others, as the above poem suggests, are not. Some people actually do collect miniature zoo animals and different colors of argyle socks. Here are some more ideas to get your creative juices flowing.

> *Coin collection:* Coin collecting does not seem quite as fun today as it did when I was little because the old silver coins are rarely found in circulation. In the days before multimetal coins, you could find a quarter that was decades old in your change from the grocery store.
>
> However, collecting coins can still be an interesting pastime for young people. Kids can try to collect a complete set of every type of coin that has been minted and in

circulation for the past twenty or so years. Most hobby or coin stores will have the books in which you store the coins and record your progress. Or, you can simply have children look through your coins to find any from the year they were born. They may want to keep these birth-year coins in a piggy bank or other safe place.

Stamp collection: Like coin collecting, stamp collecting can be a very interesting hobby for children. They can purchase a book showing a photo of each American stamp printed within the last few years. Then they can search for each stamp. You can give them envelopes with cancelled stamps to help them with their collection. Perhaps their grandparents can send them stamps they may have from years ago.

Rock or shell collection: Your child may have an interest in becoming a rock hound or beach hound, searching deserts, fields, and shorelines for varieties of rocks or shells. There are fascinating books, which not only display the different types of rocks and shells but also explain how they were formed and where the kids might find them.

Baseball card collection: Just think how much your old Babe Ruth baseball card would be worth today if you had only held on to it. Or maybe Mickey Mantle is more in your era. In any case, kids who have an interest in baseball will probably greatly enjoy starting a collection with the goal of acquiring the cards of all major league players currently in the American and National Leagues.

A collection based on the child's interests: What is your child most interested in? Maybe they have a fascination for airplanes. Start an airplane collection. Or maybe it's dolls, comic books, cars, boats, or music boxes.

Some children will start a collection on their own by trying to find different representations of their favorite animals. Cats and dogs are probably the most commonly collected, whether they are made of ceramic, rubber, plastic, or any other type of material. However, some kids collect pigs, coyotes, alligators, and even armadillos! Whatever the item, you can help the child turn the collecting process into an activity that is fun and educational.

34 ▲ Interior Decorator

The Idea: As the various holidays, seasons, and family events roll around, put your kids in charge of decorating the home (along with your help). Together you can shop for decorations or make creative decorations of your own. In addition to decorating the interior of your house, think about decorating your mailbox or porch for each special occasion.

Holiday Decor: You can decorate your home for almost any holiday that comes along. Here are decorating suggestions for Easter and Christmas and for a holiday you may have never considered.

> *Easter:* Here are some ideas for decorating your home at Easter time.

- Cut out large pieces of paper in the shapes of eggs and color them.
- Decorate Easter baskets with different colors for each room in the house
- Place Easter lilies in vases in your home.
- Spend an evening dying Easter eggs.

- Find pictures of bunnies or stuffed bunnies to put in the windows.
- Consider buying a real bunny!
- Make pretty signs with glitter or paints saying, "He is risen!"

Christmas: Here are some ideas aside from the obvious one of decorating the tree.

- Make your own tree ornaments.
- Cut out the words *Merry Christmas* using red and green paper, and display the greeting in your front window.
- Using a refrigerator carton and paint, make a cardboard cutout to stand up in your front lawn (a snowman, Santa, or sleigh).
- Construct a manger scene for your front yard.

Grandparents' Day: Have you ever seen anyone decorate for Grandparents' Day? Why not have the kids think up some clever decorations for Grandparents' Day and then invite the grandparents over. Consider one of the following ideas to get you started.

- Get a poster-sized photo of grandma and grandpa for display.
- Create big signs that say, "We love Grandpa." "We love Grandma."
- Cut out big hearts in different colors and write messages of love on them. Hang them on the walls all over the house.

- Put a sign out on the front yard that says, "Edythe Fae is the best grandmother in the world."

In addition to decorating for Grandparents' Day, see if you and your kids can think of other obscure holidays to prepare decorations for. Perhaps Groundhog Day? Or Columbus Day? You may also want to consider ways to decorate simply for the season rather than the specific holiday: pumpkins and colored leaves in the fall, flowers in the spring, birds in the summer.

Fantasy Room: Your kids can decorate their own rooms with various themes regardless of the holiday or time of the year. Perhaps one of the following ideas will be fun for your child.

- Make the kids' room look like a castle.
- Decorate it like Oz and then rent the movie.
- Have a Cowboy and Indian theme.

35 ▲ Be a Good Sport

The Idea: While your kids are still young, pick a sport you've always wanted to get involved in and learn it with them. It is unlikely that you will be able to participate together in team sports, so I recommend selecting a sport played by individuals.

Sporting Goods: There are many different sports you could learn to do with your child. I have selected a few that can be learned at almost any age. Sure, if you had started playing these sports as a teenager, you might be playing in international tournaments by now. But just think, there's still the seniors tour.

Golf: It is never too late to start playing golf, a game that is certainly cross-generational. A person could golf with a grandson and son and all come out with fairly even scores. Whether you golf in the 70s or in the 120s, your partners can be equally as good or marginal as you—no matter what their age. Golf is a relaxing game that generates camaraderie, conversation, and good outdoor fun.

Tennis: Tennis is a game that can also be learned at almost any age, although youth is a definite advantage. I've followed Jimmy Conners and Chris Evert throughout their careers (being the same age) and proudly watched them compete with teenagers well into their mid-thirties. Even if you're older than we are, you can still take a tennis class with your kids. You can even take a class as a family.

Bowling: While some would not consider bowling a physical sport, it is certainly a fun way for a family to spend time together. Some bowling alleys use the phrase, "the family who plays together stays together." Give bowling a try for a few weeks. If you begin to enjoy it, consider entering the family as a team in a local bowling league.

While individual sports may be most appropriate, you may be able to play on the same slow pitch, basketball, or volleyball team with your son or daughter. Being an adult shouldn't mean we quit playing sports. It just means we should be more mature when we lose. Remember that next time someone one-third your age beats you on the golf course or tennis court.

36 ▲ Happy Birthday Baby

The Idea: As your child's birthday approaches, think of ways to make it a very special day. And then next year, try to outdo this year's celebration.

Week-long Celebration: Start celebrating your child's birthday one week before the actual day. Each day throughout the week, plan for a different special event. Here are some ideas for those special events.

A party a day: Plan on having several parties throughout the week. One could be just for family, another for the kids at school, and one for the kids on the soccer team or girl scout troop. Still another celebration could be at brunch after church with friends from Sunday school. Perhaps you could hold this party at your child's favorite restaurant.

A gift a day: Surprise your child a week before his or her birthday by giving a gift. Then each day before the event give another. On the birthday give the best gift of all. The gifts do not need to be expensive.

You may want to have all the gifts interrelate. For example, if you are giving a train set, give him or her one car per day with the track given on the birthday. Or give sets of doll clothes and accessories first and the doll on the birthday.

A card a day: In addition to giving your child a card on the birthday, give a card each day of the week before. You can make them yourself. Put one in the lunch box on Monday, in the coat pocket on Tuesday, on the pillow on Wednesday, and so on throughout the week.

Special excursions: Take your child on a different excursion every day. Maybe he or she is a movie buff. Take him or her to the movies several nights that week. Or maybe your child would like to go to a different ice cream parlor every night. You may want to consider other ideas in this book to give you birthday-week excursion options.

With a Song in Your Heart: Consider rewriting the words to a song for your child. You can make the song funny, a brief history of his or her life, or use your own imagination in other ways. If you don't feel you have the creativity to rewrite the words to a song, ask one of your creative friends to help you.

Theme Party: If the above idea of one party per night for a week overwhelms you, consider throwing a big party in honor of your child centered around a certain theme. You can have the kids all dress in costumes for a "Sesame Street" party or a *Wizard of Oz* party. Or, you can have the gifts create the theme. You might ask each person to bring a stuffed animal for Caitlin, who wants to expand her collection, or something to do with baseball for Patrick, who is an avid Dodger fan.

The Big Day: Make your child feel very special on his or her birthday. Maybe you could give him or her a card to open every hour throughout the day. From dawn to bedtime, see how many times you can give the birthday boy or girl a hug, a gift, or an I-love-you greeting.

37 ▲ Go Fly a Kite

The Idea: Gather your kids together and spend a morning or afternoon at the park or beach flying kites.

Preparing for the Day: Start this day of activity by purchasing a kite or two. If you reflect on your childhood, this may sound like an easy task. But today there are almost as many varieties of kites as there are species of birds.

If you live near a big city, you may be able to find a store that sells nothing but kites. There are many such shops in specialty malls and shopping centers. You may choose to buy an elaborate kite with multiple sections or one with more than one string. If you and your kids are novices, you might want to start with a basic four-sided kite. Be sure to buy kite string while you're shopping.

Flying the Kite: The kids will be counting on you to know just the right weather and wind speed for ideal kite flying. While you may not be an expert, you should be sure there is a mild wind blowing. Otherwise your kite will get no further in the air than your height on tiptoe plus the length of the kite.

Trust me. If the air is dead calm, pick another way to have fun with your kids from this book. Save kite flying for the appropriate weather.

Topics for Discussion: While flying your kite you may want to discuss the principles of flying with your child. Or you may want to explain Ben Franklin's experiment. Perhaps you can discuss the history of kite flying. Of course, you should probably spend time together with an encyclopedia or at the local library to learn as much as you can about kites.

Additional Experiments: Did you ever send a message up your kite when you were a little kid? If you did, you might remember how to do it. If you didn't, simply take a circular piece of paper and cut a hole in the middle. The paper should look somewhat like a flat doughnut. Place the kite string through the hole in the piece of paper. The wind should carry the paper most of the way up the string and in some cases all the way to your kite. If it doesn't work, try using lighter or heavier paper or pieces of paper of different sizes.

Another trick is to make a big spider, or other object, out of lightweight Styrofoam. Once your kite is well in the air, tie your spider to a piece of fishing line about six feet long. Then tie the other end of the fishing line to your kite string just beyond your hand. (You will probably need help so the kite doesn't get away.) Let out some of your kite string so the spider moves away from you.

If the wind is right and your spider is the proper weight, the spider should be suspended in the air not too far above the ground. People walking by will be wondering how such a thing could float in thin air.

Kite Flying Contest: If you want to include the whole neighborhood, hold your own kite flying contest. Announce to the kids you will be giving a small prize for the highest flying kite, the most colorful kite, and the most extravagant kite. Then ask your neighbors to help you judge.

Happy Endings: Many kids never see their kite again once they've flown it high in the sky. Sometimes kids are not able to hold on to the string the whole time, and the kite flies away. Other times the string breaks during an unexpected gust. If your child is able to retrieve his or her kite, you will have a happy ending. If the kite is lost in some way, offer the child this consolation. "Maybe your kite decided to move on so that some other little boy or girl could have as much fun as you did." That might satisfy your child if they're sad about losing the kite. But you can always go with them to select a bigger and fancier kite for your next outing!

38 ▲ Rock Out

The Idea: Popular music plays an important part in the lives of kids today. As a parent, youth pastor, or other significant adult, you should show interest in their music. Even if it's tough to do, try to enjoy the music they listen to (assuming the lyrics are in good taste), and perhaps you can "rock out" with your kids.

Attend a Rock Concert: While I would never recommend that you attend a concert (or allow your kids to listen to a group) with music and lyrics that are offensive to you, I do suggest that you find some common ground. Maybe there is a group your kids listen to that you can tolerate. Or perhaps, by some fluke, your kids like the old group that is in town on its comeback tour. And, before you completely throw away the idea of attending your kids' choice of concerts, consider taking along ear plugs.

Lip Sync: When the family is together, or when a group of kids is just sitting around, consider this idea for lots of laughs. First, find something that resembles a microphone. Next, have each person select a song from your collection of albums, tapes, or CDs.

As your song is played, move your lips to the singer's words. The bigger the ham, the more fun. You will have even more fun if other people lip sync for the backup vocalists. If there are no lyrics to some of the songs selected, have people play imaginary instruments.

Song Party: Throw a party for your child, telling each person invited that he or she must come as a song. You'll be surprised at the imaginary costumes people will create. Can you imagine someone coming as "Somewhere over the Rainbow," "How Much Is That Doggie in the Window," or "Greensleeves"? If each person keeps the song title a secret, you can have a game to see who guesses the most songs correctly. Or, you can give awards for the best costume.

Sing-along: Hold a gathering where musically talented members of the family play the piano or guitar while everyone else sings along. You can sing as a group and also have each person sing a solo. Don't worry about how well you sing. The fun is in the trying.

There are many records or tapes you can purchase for children of all ages that are made for sing-alongs. Buy some of these for the home or car and make time to have regular songfests.

39 ▲ A Book Case

The Idea: Help your children create a library of their own. Like the public library, your children's books can be arranged using a numbering system, or you can create sections for each different type of book.

Some Topics to Consider: Every child has different interests, so every child's library can be unique. Here are categories you might consider as you build a library for your child.

Storybooks: In this section you can build up a collection of your child's favorite children's stories. Almost every child has two or three favorite books that are taken everywhere.

Favorite authors: If he or she enjoys the stories of a particular author, such as Dr. Seuss, Beatrix Potter or A. A. Milne, you may want to reserve a special shelf for such books. You may even want to consider decorating your child's room around the theme and central characters of a favorite story.

Books for learning: As your child gets older you may want to start buying him or her books that help identify animals, the alphabet, and then more complicated words and concepts.

Books on hobbies: If your child is fascinated with race cars, begin to buy a lot of books about cars. If he or she loves roller skating, begin to collect books about this sport.

Bible stories: Consider making a section of your child's library especially for a Bible and any books containing Bible stories for children.

Books on "fun": Find other books in addition to this one that will give you and your child ideas about having fun together. Add them to your library too.

Finding Books: There are thousands of children's books currently in book stores. To find out what your child's taste in books is, spend time with your child at the public library. Find out what books he or she takes off the shelf. Ask why that particular book was selected.

If your budget does not allow much book buying, you might find book bargains at libraries that sell to the public used or donated duplicate books. You can also find some great deals on used children's books at garage sales or rummage sales.

40 ▲ Hook, Line, and Sinker

The Idea: Some of the best adult-child bonding comes during times like fishing trips. While waiting for the fish to bite, talk with one another about anything and everything—even fish.

Scouting a Location: The first thing you need to do is to decide what type of fishing you're going to try. Unless you live on the coast, you are probably limited to freshwater fishing. Those near the coast have the option of a saltwater excursion. You must also decide whether to

- go out on a boat or fish from the shore.
- fish from a pier.
- fish for trout or go for the marlin.

The Gear: If you are an experienced fisherman, you probably have your own fishing poles and tackle. If you are going deep-sea fishing, or if you are going to a place where fishing is a prominent sport, you will probably be able to rent the gear. In most states you will be required to get a fishing license also.

The Fishing Trip: In keeping with the "simple" theme of this book, you may want to find a place near your home where kids can catch fish from a stocked stream or lake. If you've never gone fishing before, this would be my recommendation. However, if you have fished before, or if you can bring along someone who is an experienced fisherman, I recommend the following for perfect fishing, relaxation, and fun with your child.

- Find a mountain lake surrounded by big pine trees on a day when the sun is shining, but the temperature isn't too hot. That way, if the fishing isn't too good, you and your child will still be able to appreciate the beauty of nature.
- Rent a rowboat large enough for the people involved. In addition to the gear, take some cushions for comfort in case you decide to stay out all day. Pack a picnic lunch to take out on the lake with you.
- Help your children bait the hook. If they do actually catch something, be there to see the joy on their faces. It could well be a moment they will remember for the rest of their lives.
- Ask the kids how they are doing in school. Look at the wonders of God's creation around you. Laugh with one another. Try out some outrageous puns. Even if you don't catch a thing, you are sure to have a day of fellowship and fun.

41 ▲ Something's Fishy

The Idea: If you don't care to hook 'em, look 'em. Take your kids to see fish at a local aquatic park, fish store, or consider keeping your own aquarium.

Eye the Fish: Children love watching fish. Whether it's the goldfish they won at the ball toss during the last church festival, or the great whales that migrate each winter, your child should enjoy any opportunity to observe aquatic life. Here are some ways to view the underwater world.

> *Aquatic parks:* It used to be that aquatic parks were located only near the coastline. However, there are now parks with very large dolphin, whale, and sea lion shows in various places throughout the country. Many major cities that do not yet have a large aquatic park do have aquariums that allow people to view the undersea world from beneath the water's surface. Find the nearest aquarium or park and plan to visit soon.

Snorkeling: If you are afraid to try snorkeling in clear water, I have a one-word suggestion for you. Reconsider! There are few things more fascinating than the many different species of colorful animals beneath the surface of our oceans. Though your kids may have some fears when they first put on a snorkel and mask, chances are that once they've made that first dive, you'll have trouble keeping them out of the water. Dive with them on a future vacation. Explore new things together.

Hands on: Another way to have fun with our slippery friends is to help your child keep an aquarium. You can share this hobby with one another. Like your fishing decision, you can decide whether to keep fresh or saltwater fish.

You should start off small for at least two reasons. First, you will want to learn how to care for fish without risking the lives of too many fish or risking too much of your budget. Second, you want to make sure the hobby is one that will last. The last thing you want to do is buy a two-hundred-gallon fish tank only to have both you and your child lose interest in the third month.

As you buy each new fish and graduate to the next size of aquarium, take time to learn about each species. If you start with a saltwater tank, you can progressively expand from an aquarium filled with only fish to one that has dozens of varieties of living coral, sea urchins, and anemones. You can even have shrimp or sea horses.

42 ▲ Fun Factory

The Idea: Do a little research to see what major manufacturing or food service companies are nearby. See if you can arrange for a tour of the facility. Focus upon tours that would be interesting or fun for the kids, rather than those that would be of most interest to you.

Factory Ideas: While a factory tour may sound boring, many kids are fascinated to see the automation and steps that are involved in producing a finished product—especially one that they are familiar with. Here are some industries that might be of particular interest for children. Keep in mind that many factories, especially those dealing with food, give visitors free samples!

> *Chocolate factory:*   If I lived in Hershey, Pennsylvania, I'd probably weigh fifty pounds more. A chocolate company there has a great public tour of its facility. If you don't live anywhere near Pennsylvania, you can probably find a chocolate factory

somewhere near you, if you look hard enough.

Bakery: The next best thing to a chocolate factory is a bakery. You might be able to see bakers make pies, cookies, and other goodies.

Beverage bottler: What ingredients go in to making your child's favorite beverage? Perhaps there is a bottling plant for one of the major soft drinks near your home.

Dairy: While a dairy may not be considered a factory, a visit should be considered because of the many steps involved in making a bottle of pasteurized milk.

Toy factory: While any samples on this factory tour won't be edible, your kids will benefit greatly from seeing how some of their favorite toys are designed, molded, packaged, and distributed.

Car, airplane, or boat manufacturer: If you have the chance to take your child through a plant that assembles cars, trucks, airplanes, or boats, follow through on the idea. You will be amazed at how many parts go into making a single vehicle.

Perhaps none of these factories are near your home. Instead you have factories that manufacture rivets, paper towels, and electrical components. So what! You'd be surprised at how fascinated a child can be watching raw materials transformed so quickly into a product he or she uses every day.

43 ▲ A Real Trooper

The Idea: There are a great number of organizations you could join, or athletic activities you could coach, to give you more time with your child. Here are suggestions of things you can do not only with your kids but together with other kids and their parents.

Be a Leader: If your child is interested in joining Cub Scouts, Girl Scouts, Boy Scouts, or Brownies, consider being a den mother or father. Not only will you get more time to have fun with your kids, but you will be with other kids as well. If you don't have time to become a leader for one of these groups, try to take as much interest as possible in what your kids are doing. If they have camping trips, do whatever you can to join them. If they need parent volunteers for an event, be ready to give your time.

Parent and Child Groups: There are a number of organizations that are designed for parents and children to participate together. In the Indian Y-Guides and Indian Princesses programs of the YMCA, fathers and sons or fathers and daughters meet together for a time of sharing, crafts, and community service projects. It's a great way for you to watch your child grow and for you both to develop new friendships with the other members of the group.

Sports Team: Are your children interested in any sports? Next season, instead of dropping them off for little league or soccer practice, consider becoming one of the coaches or team managers. Not only will you be an inspiration for your son or daughter, but you may help other children on the team, especially those who lack a mom or dad at home.

In addition to the coaching idea, you may be able to find a club or gym in your area that encourages family swim teams or bike rides for fun and relaxation.

Big Brother or Big Sister: Perhaps you know a lonely child or a child without one or both parents. Include this child in some of the activities you do with your own children or youth group. Perhaps you know of a child who is rejected by peers or a child new to the area. Include him or her in your group.

Camp Counselor: Consider becoming a camp counselor for your church, community, or YMCA. Young peoples' lives can be changed drastically in one week or weekend because a camp counselor took the time to listen, teach, and care.

In many communities, there are day camps held during various times of the year. If you don't have time to counsel at a week-long camp, often there is a need for adult volunteers for these day-long events.

Sunday School: Consider becoming a volunteer teacher at church for the upcoming school year or summer term. You may also be needed as a volunteer for activities for a vacation Bible school program. Even if you don't have children of your own, but love spending time with kids, this is a great opportunity for involvement.

44 ▲ Park Place

The Idea: There are many different kinds of parks where you can go to have fun with your children—from the park down the street to the great national parks. Enjoying our country's parks can also be the opportunity to encourage your kids to help the environment by keeping parks clean and litter-free.

The Park Down the Street: As often as possible take your kids to the local parks in your city. Perhaps there is one within walking distance of your home. Try to go to a variety of parks in your area. Your children may find that they like the slide at one park, the hillsides at another, and the open field in still another. Here are some activities you can do once you are at the park.

> *Playground equipment:* Next time your kids want to swing, get on the swing next to them. They will love seeing you enjoy the same kind of fun they enjoy. Next, go over to the merry-go-round and give the kids a spin. Perhaps there will be a slide and other

play equipment for you to help them climb and ride.

Walk: Take walks around the perimeter of the park, talking with your child about all the different sights, smells, and sounds. Try to notice the little things such as the butterfly drifting by or the bee visiting the flowers for pollen.

Take a picnic: You don't have to plan a day-long excursion just to have a picnic. You can make some sandwiches, grab a blanket, and go to the local park for a picnic whenever the weather permits. Before eating you can lie on the blanket and relax with the kids.

Games: Throw a Frisbee to one another. Play catch with a football. Bring a croquet set with you. Some parks may have basketball courts, tetherball areas, or shuffleboard. Try them all.

Amusement Parks: Chances are that somewhere within a day's journey there is an amusement park that your kids will enjoy. People in southern California have many amusement parks to choose from. If Disneyland is not in your backyard, consider taking your children to the closest park that has rides, entertainers, and games. If there is no permanent amusement park nearby, take your kids to the local county fair or other annual carnival event.

National Park:　If you have never visited our national parks, you are missing some of the most beautiful scenery in the world. From Yellowstone to Bryce Canyon to Great Smoky Mountains National Park, each park contains a different beauty and magic, making our country among the prettiest in the world.

Plan a vacation to take your children to as many national parks as possible. While there, travel the many hiking trails. Read about the history of the park. Try to view the sunset or sunrise from spectacular vantage points. See how many different animals you can spot along the way. Take lots of pictures. The state of Utah alone could fill your vacation schedule for the next several years. It has many beautiful national parks.

Spend time with your children while they are young. Whether you are able to go with them to the great national parks, or make only an occasional trip to the park down the street, the kids will know you care enough about them to share big and little adventures.

45 ▲ Gobble, Gobble

The Idea: Make Thanksgiving more than just a day when the kids get to see their cousins or the neighbors down the street. Ask them to help you with the day by participating in one or all of the following ways.

Cooking the Meal: Ask the kids to help you with part of the meal. Perhaps they might enjoy mashing the potatoes or baking the rolls.

Reading the Story of the Pilgrims: Perhaps this year before you sit down for Thanksgiving dinner, one of the children in your group could read an abbreviated account of the first Thanksgiving. Some of the adults may even learn a thing or two.

Starting a New Tradition: Consider doing something different this Thanksgiving. For over thirty years as I was growing up my family went to the mountains for the Thanksgiving weekend. The trip became a tradition and was the one weekend a year completely devoted to spending time with each other. Your new tradition may be something as simple as the reading of the story mentioned above.

Decorating the Room: There are several things the kids can do to have fun on Thanksgiving and to make your day more special.

> *Make place cards:* Spend the time with the kids to make place cards for the dinner table displaying the Thanksgiving theme and each person's name. They could make miniature cardboard turkeys to hold each person's place card.

> *Create a centerpiece:* Early in the day, join the kids to create a centerpiece for the Thanksgiving dinner table. Let them use their imagination or provide them with suggestions.

> *Ask them to pray:* As you sit down for the Thanksgiving meal, ask one or all of the children to give the blessing, thanking God for all that He has provided for the family. Some families sing a song of thanksgiving together as their prayer.

Express Your Thankfulness: Thanksgiving is an opportune time not only to have fun with your kids but to affirm them as individuals. Sometime during the Thanksgiving dinner, go around the room and ask each person to mention reasons why they are thankful.

46 ▲ Where We Stop Nobody Knows

The Idea: Plan a mystery day. It can be a day of mystery to the kids. It can be a day of mystery to you. Or, it can be a mysterious day to everyone concerned. Often the days with the least structure are the days with the most unexpected fun!

A Mystery to the Kids: This book has presented many different ideas for excursions with your kids. While most of the time you will share your plans with the kids, consider having a few surprise excursions each year. Your surprise may be as simple as a short trip to the ice cream store or as expensive as a weekend in the mountains at a rented cabin.

Everyone likes surprises. Kids like them even more if the activity you've planned is something *they* like to do. If visiting Uncle George makes your child break out in hives, I wouldn't recommend it as your surprise excursion.

A Mystery to You: Let the kids take you on a surprise excursion. Tell them that you will be prepared to take them anywhere they want to go for the day (within easy driving distance and according to a predetermined budget).

Aside from asking the kids what kind of clothes you should wear, don't ask them anything about the trip until you get in the car and start driving. If your kids are special, maybe they'll offer to treat you to the entire day, and you won't have to worry about bringing money!

A Mystery to All: Have you ever had a day when nothing was planned, and it surprisingly turned out to be one of the most fun days you've ever had? There are several ways you could implement this mystery day.

>   *Just go!* To make this a mystery day for all, get in the car, or on bikes, or on the bus and simply start traveling. Consider taking a route that is new to you, heading in a direction that you rarely travel. If something looks interesting to someone along the way, stop and decide if that is a place where you want to spend some time. Otherwise, keep going.
>   You may simply find a new restaurant that everyone enjoys. On the other hand, you may end up participating in a fun activity that is new and exciting for everyone involved. Give it a try. You may be in for a big surprise, especially if you're the personality

type that has to have every moment carefully planned.

Five ideas each: Have each person going on the surprise excursion write down five activities they'd like to do that day. Put all the ideas into a hat and have someone draw the winning idea. If it is suitable for the group, keep the destination a secret until it becomes obvious to everyone where you are headed.

One of 52:   Consider taking this book and randomly opening it to any page. Then use the idea described there for your surprise excursion. If the idea you pick is one for the home, try opening the book a second time. Or like the idea above, write a dozen ideas from this book on separate sheets of paper. Then randomly pick one from a hat for your surprise excursion.

47 ▲ Snow Use

The Idea: Spend a day in the snow with your children. It's easy if you live in Buffalo, New York or Aspen, Colorado. If you live in sunny southern California, however, this may seem like an impractical idea. Yet, chances are you could find a place where the snow falls within a day's drive of home.

Things to Do: There are a great deal of things you can do with the kids in the snow. You'll probably have the most fun with them, however, if you act like a kid yourself. Here are a few ideas.

> *Build a snowman:* No activity in the snow is more fun than building a snowman. Build one together as a family or group. Use a variety of objects for the eyes, nose, ears, hat, and other features. Try making snowpeople that look like members of your group.

> *Take a hike:* Perhaps there is an area near where you live or where you visit that features a pleasant path. If you're lucky you can take your walk during a snowfall when

the snowflakes are as big as quarters and the wind is completely still. Bundle up warm, put on your mittens, and enjoy each other's company.

Go skiing: While skiing isn't meant for everyone, you may enjoy taking the kids with you on your next trip. Maybe you haven't skied in years. Maybe it's time to begin again.

Sledding: How long has it been since you rode on a sled, toboggan, or innertube? This year rather than watching with a parental eye that imagines every sled hitting a tree, ride with the kids. Then you can hit the tree, too!

Make snow angels: Perhaps your kids have never made a snow angel before. Find an area where the snow is deep and level. Lie on your back with your arms straight out to your side. Move your arms up and down like a bird trying to fly. Stand up carefully and see the wonderful outlines of snow angels.

Have a snowball fight: Find soft snow so that no one gets hurt. When your target least expects it, throw it his or her way. Just be sure you can still outrun the target! Or, you might be sorry—and wet!

48 ▲ Scavenger Hunt

The Idea: Make a list of various and sundry items the kids should be able to find around the house. Send them on a scavenger hunt to find as many of the objects as possible. You can either send them out in the neighborhood, or you can save this idea for a rainy day and give them something to do around the house.

Setting the Rules: Before turning your kids loose on their hunt, you should establish rules such as:

- A time limit of one or two hours (or more depending on how complicated you make the list)
- Boundaries (you may want them to search within your own house and garage or allow them to stay only on your block)
- No purchase rule (they must find these objects, not purchase them)

Making the List: Your scavenger hunt will be a lot more fun if you use as much variety as possible in creating your list of items to collect. Make some items a bit more challenging, but don't add items that will be impossible to find. Here are things you may want to include in your list.

A red button
A piece of yellow rope
A daisy
A deck of cards with both jokers
A magazine with a picture of a turtle
A 1975 penny
A newspaper ad for furniture
A used airline ticket
Chopsticks
A used Christmas card
A toy soldier

A Reward: Before you implement this idea be sure you've already purchased or arranged for some kind of award to give to your kids when they complete the task. Even if they were not able to find all the items on the scavenger hunt list, give them a prize anyway.

An Alternative: Consider this alternative type of scavenger hunt for your kids, depending on their age. This idea requires that you borrow or purchase a camera that provides instant pictures and a couple of rolls of film. Rather than having the kids find objects, you have them take pictures of certain things or people.

49 ▲ 'Tis the Season

The Idea: While you probably have many traditions of your own at Christmas, I wanted to give you special ideas not only for having fun with your kids but for bringing some fun to other kids' lives.

Deck the Halls: In the chapter "Interior Decorator" I suggested ways to decorate your home for the holidays, including having your children make their own ornaments for the tree. When it comes time for the tree decorating ceremony, try to make sure your entire family or group is together. Busy schedules too often conflict with special times like these. Set a special day or evening for the ceremony and ask everyone to keep their calendars clear.

Here We Go a Caroling: Gather a group of friends or a group of families and go out caroling. Have each person carry a candle and serenade your neighbors. Consider going to a convalescent home or hospital to bring joy to people who may not be home for the holidays. If you're unable to do this, consider singing carols in your home as you decorate the tree.

Turn on the Lights: Take the kids out to see the lights of the city. Perhaps there is a neighborhood near you that goes all out each year with various displays on lawns and lights on the houses. If not, consider joining with your neighbors to make your block the one everyone else comes to see.

Keep Those Cards and Letters Coming: This year, instead of spending lots of money buying Christmas cards from the store, have your kids custom make each one using a wide variety of arts and crafts. Use a folded sheet of colored construction paper and have them draw a picture on the outside and write a warm greeting on the inside. Then you can finish it off with your personal greeting and signature. You can also use white paper with watercolors or rubber stamps.

Santa Claus Is Coming to Town: Help your small children write a letter to Santa Claus and have them hand deliver it to the man himself at a local mall. This way you can find out what gifts they want and get your traditional picture of the kids and Santa at the same time. You can also help the children prepare a plate of food for Santa and the reindeer on Christmas Eve.

Movie Time: To get you in the Christmas spirit, rent one of the traditional great Christmas movies or programs for the family to view together. I recommend *Miracle on 34th Street* or *It's a Wonderful Life.* Or shorter programs for the kids like "Rudolph the Red-Nosed Reindeer" or "How the Grinch Stole Christmas."

It Is More Blessed to Give: Help your children learn the true meaning of Christmas this year by teaching them to give to children less fortunate than they are. Perhaps you know a family whose father is in prison or whose mother has died in the past year. Maybe the family is too sad or financially insecure to prepare for Christmas.

Consider bringing the family a tree, complete with lights and ornaments. Buy each of the kids a present that your children have picked out. Invite them over for Christmas dinner or bring them a turkey for a special dinner in their own home.

Consider calling your local social services department or a local rescue mission. They may be able to tell you where the help is needed most. As a family, you may decide to help an agency prepare and serve a holiday meal.

The Christmas Story: Sometime during the season gather the family or group together and tell the story of the young virgin girl who rode into a town called Bethlehem on a donkey, accompanied by her faithful husband, Joseph. Describe how the baby Jesus was born into the world in a stable, surrounded by animals, and placed to sleep in a pile of straw. It's a story children love to hear year after year.

50 ▲ Day in and Day out

The Idea: Most of the ideas in this book suggest ways for you to spend an afternoon, evening, or whole day with your children having fun. In addition to such planned activities, spend time each and every day with your kids, either helping them learn something new or doing something fun, even if it is only for a few minutes.

Here are some ideas of everyday things you can do to have fun with your child.

- Take a daily walk with your children.
- Read a story to them.
- Take them to the market with you.
- Hold a gourmet dinner party for your kids and their friends.
- Designate a week with no television and a different activity each night.
- Pick wild berries.
- Crack and hull nuts for cooking.
- Color in their coloring books with them.
- Make your own miniature golf course inside your house.
- Rake leaves and then jump in them.

- Roast marshmallows.
- Carve pumpkins.
- Go out to an entertaining pizza restaurant.
- Pay a surprise visit to family friends together.
- If you are going on a trip, bring a gift for the kids to open every one hundred miles.
- Learn some card tricks together.
- Ask the kids what they'd like to do, then do it.
- Blow bubbles.
- Try to find shapes of objects or animals within the clouds.
- Watch cartoons together.
- Ask "what if" questions.
- Make different costumes at home or dress up in old clothes.
- Teach them a new game.
- Sit by them when they're sick.
- Help them with their homework.
- Read the funnies together.
- Just sit and talk about school or events in the neighborhood.

II

Just Say No
to Watching T.V.

To
our dear friends

Warren (Bear) and Jan Moseley

Thanks for pushing my wife
out into that aisle
—I'm forever indebted!

▲ Contents

▲ Introduction

Your children have a unique opportunity to spend close to fifteen thousand hours before the age of seven doing what they'll dream of being able to do the rest of their lives: playing.

Play is children's work. It is the way they explore the world.

Play is a state of mind—a view of the world that says, "I'm curious," "I want to know more," "I'd like to know why," and "I can have fun figuring out life and meeting new people and exploring new ideas."

Play is involvement with the world—sometimes with other children and sometimes with adults. It provides a means of learning how to cope with or conquer life's problems and how to converse, make decisions, and solve problems with life's co-travelers.

Play is the way children figure out how things work and what is most rewarding to them personally.

Much of what adults might call building, expressing, learning, experimenting, creating, or working is what children would call having fun or playing.

The greatest thief of playtime is television. It literally robs your children of experiences that will fashion their lives, expand their minds and hearts, and add layers upon layers of depth and character to their personalities. Stated another way, *the greatest enemy to their potential is television.*

What does television give to children in place of their creativity and energy? Prepackaged story lines. Commercials. A hefty dose of violence. A skewed view of sexual relationships and the role of children in our society. And a lot of frenetic music accompanying a blur of meaningless motion programmed in such a way that children begin to see all of life in eight- to ten-minute time spans. Not only does television rob something precious from your children. It leaves a cheap, hollow substitute for real life in its place.

Your children will experience a better quality of life if you will limit their viewing of carefully selected television programs and videotapes to no more than four hours a week.

"But what can I encourage my kids to do instead of watch TV?" you may ask.

Here are some suggestions.

1 ▲ Reading

In the opinion of most parents I've asked, the number one preferred alternative activity to watching television for their children is reading.

Why Read? Reading does several things far better than television:

- *Reading stimulates creativity.* Children must think the details of a scene or a character, even though a description may be provided by a book—thus envisioning clothing, facial gestures, sound of voice, surrounding environments, and action. What they envision is invariably far richer in detail and depth of characterization than are the images presented on most children's programs.
- *Reading stimulates problem-solving and decision-making skills.* Children learn how to develop reasoning ability as they read. The unfolding plot of a book invites the question, What do you think will happen next? For viewers of television, that question is resolved too quickly to engage a response.
- *Reading allows children to absorb a story at*

their own pace. Time-outs can be taken for daydreaming. The story can be picked up and put down at will. Children have control over the story—rather than the television set dictating the pace of action. Furthermore, they can reread a story as often as they like.

• *Reading helps children develop language ability.* Children learn new vocabulary words as they read. They encounter various patterns of sentence construction and the wonderful worlds of rhyme and alliteration. They learn the fine art of verbal jokes—puns and witticisms. They learn to distinguish characters by the words they speak rather than the way they look; they develop an understanding that people are more than their appearance. Children follow a line of reasoning far more clearly in print than on videotape. And in following a line of reasoning, they are learning to reason. Finally, children are given far more clues about a character's motivations and inner thought life and feelings in books than on TV.

• *Reading separates a story line from commercial messages.* The result is a seamless story, unpunctuated by product pitches. It follows that comprehension of the story is better when the story is read than when it is seen.

How to Choose?   In choosing books for your children or in helping older children select books, consider these points:

1. Make certain the book is a challenge at, or slightly beyond, the individual's reading level. The book must not be too difficult to read, however. Children should be challenged to learn several new words with each book.

2. Make certain the book is in line with the values you are hoping to instill. A number of children's books emphasize ghosts, goblins, monsters, and other fantasy creatures.

3. Some books are based on television programs or children's movies. In other cases, the books were classics first, and the media version followed. By letting your children read the book version of a popular story, you are helping them engage in a common experience with peers, yet without the extra doses of violence often included in the movie version.

Read Together   Reading is an activity that unites parents and children. Read to your children. (Even older children will enjoy a book read by a parent for a few minutes a day.) Ask them to read to you. Make books a part of your conversations. Go to the library together each week. Build a library for your children of favorite, traditional, beautifully illustrated, and best-loved books. It will be a treasure they will value even more as the years go by.

2 ▲ "Make-Believe" Play

Encourage your children to make up story lines and to act out the plots they create:

- Make up characters.
- Give both voice and words to characters.
- Adopt mannerisms and costumes for the characters.
- Create sets or "stages" on which their characters might act out dramas.
- Engage in action sequences.

Exploration Make-believe play isn't designed for performance or for review by adults (although the wise parent occasionally will unobtrusively watch kids at such play for signs of aggressive or inappropriate behavior). This play is simply for children's pleasure in exploring the world.

Children must be taught to play in this way. Sit down with them periodically and help them make up stories using toy props. Teach them how characters engage in dialogue. Give them ideas for a setting, such as a fort made from a card table, a roadway made from lined-up blocks, or an entire house contained in a bedroom or outlined in the dirt outside. Prime the pump of imagination.

Role-Play Through make-believe play, children try on various roles in life. Suggest scenarios. For example, they might play "house" . . . "store" . . . "school" . . . "office" . . . "restaurant" . . . "church" (or synagogue) . . . "police station" . . . "fire station" . . . "Wild West fort" . . . "deserted island" . . . "space station" . . . "farm" . . . "ocean liner" . . . "hospital" . . . and so on. Imagination is the limit!

As they get older, encourage your children to try scenes from different time periods—colonial days, ancient times, or A.D. 2100. Encourage your children to play in a setting that might involve people of different races and cultures in a positive way. You may want to enhance the make-believe world with costumes and props in a "dress-up" trunk.

Cooperation Group make-believe play helps children learn to play in a cooperative manner. Watch them as they play in small groups. Make suggestions that will allow (1) each child to have a turn as leader or plot creator—the child who sets the parameters of the action and scene, (2) each child to have a turn playing the leading character, whether hero or villain, (3) each child to have an opportunity to take part in the action (note: every child should have speaking lines), and (4) each child to have a say in how the play develops and is finally resolved. It takes practice to learn to play in a cooperative, fuss-free manner.

Back to Reality   All is reality to a child; some children have difficulty differentiating the fantasy world of their creation from the real world. Encourage make-believe play but continually call children back to reality when playtime is over.

3 ▲ Group Games and Sports

Send your children outside to play whenever possible. Provide sporting props and they will soon find that outside action play is more fun than watching sports on TV.

Various activities are appropriate for kids:

- Baseball or softball. Or kids can play catch without bats and bases.
- Soccer. It has rapidly become the sport of choice for children under ten.
- Basketball. If you don't have a hoop, your children can set up a trash can as a goal and even substitute a soccer ball for a basketball.
- Frisbee throwing. Your children may want to make up a Frisbee "golf course" or a Frisbee version of shuffleboard.
- Foursquare or twosquare. This bouncing ball game is popular on school playgrounds.
- Croquet. Kids can adapt a baseball bat and ball for play.
- Jump rope. Lots of different jumps and related rhymes and songs are possible.
- Marbles and jacks. These games can be played indoors, too.

Nerf balls, made of Nerf foam, are good for children from young ages to teens. Play with these items results in far fewer bruises and broken windows. Nerf sets for softball, field hockey, golf, Ping-Pong, and other sports can generally be used for indoor play as well as outdoor play.

With swing sets, tetherball courts, and other outdoor activity sets (which may include slides, rope ladders, and other climbing accessories), kids can burn up excess energy.

Add a net to the play action and you can create a variety of games and sports in your yard, on your driveway, or in your apartment house parking lot or patio area, such as tennis, volleyball, badminton, a soccerball version of Ping-Pong, and other games your children create.

Advantages   Games and sports help children develop motor skills—both large muscle and small muscle—as well as hand-eye coordination. Children also learn the function of rules and concepts of fairness.

Encourage cooperative play rather than competitive play. Also encourage your children to let all playmates have a turn or be part of a team. Group games and sports teach children that not all people have equal skill levels and that one can have fun even if he isn't the biggest, fastest, or best at a sport.

Safety   The alone child can develop certain skills related to these games. A child can practice pitching into a net, chase a Frisbee all over the yard, jump rope, shoot baskets, and play marbles or jacks without a playmate.

Make certain that your children know how to use all sporting equipment safely and that they understand the "limits" of the court or playing field. Never allow them to play in the street; give them instructions about what to do if a ball sails over a fence, goes into the street, or lands in the neighbor's prized flower bed. Check out a vacant lot or playing field for gopher holes, broken bottles, and other potential hazards.

4 ▲ Cooking

Cooking is the one skill children can use all their lives. No matter what they choose as occupations, they'll always need to eat.

Basic Skills Cooking can be a parent-child activity. Even young children can measure and stir. As they mature and hand-eye coordination develops, ask them to make a salad, mix a batch of cookies, or bake a cake. Your children will take pride in a task that is accomplished successfully and will enjoy both eating the finished product and receiving the praise of family members.

Teach your children to read a recipe.

Teach them basic cooking techniques—such as how to crack open an egg, turn pancakes, and measure staples.

Teach your children how to use basic kitchen appliances and utensils, including knives. It's amazing how much they can prepare in a microwave, given a little instruction.

Let your children help you with various kitchen activities, such as sorting through the beans before soaking them.

Staying Safe   Teach your kids what to do if a fire erupts (in other words, how to use the fire extinguisher that should be located in your kitchen pantry) . . . what to do if they burn or cut themselves . . . and how to safely use an oven and a stove.

Etiquette and Economics   Show your children how to set a table properly and let that be a regular chore.

Ask your kids to help with grocery shopping. You may want to give them (ten years and older) a list of three items to find in the store while you put other things into your basket. Show them how to comparison shop, read labels, and look for bargains. Make grocery shopping a challenge and your kids will hardly notice that it's also an educational experience.

Cleanup   Finally, teach them how to clean up the kitchen and let them help you after meals.

Adventures with Foods   Your children may develop a specialty as junior chefs. One young man considers himself the best spaghetti and chili man on his block. A teenage girl has developed her own version of the best chocolate cake in the world. Your teenager may want to experiment with different types of pizzas and other put-together-with-lots-of-variety meals, such as stuffed baked potatoes, nachos, and omelettes.

Children from early ages can make sandwiches and can help with preparing school lunches.

Introduce older children to new foods, new spices and herbs, and new taste combinations. They will enjoy eating a balanced diet more if they have a part in creating it and can enhance it with spices and condiments of their choosing.

Rather than allow your kids to eat junk food in front of the tube, encourage them to create nutritious food.

5 ▲ Puzzles

Children can spend hours . . . and hours . . . and hours . . . working and reworking puzzles.

Puzzles for Tots   For the little ones, select wooden puzzles with knobs. Puzzles are made of lots of materials these days, from wood to plastic to foam to furry fabric. Your children can explore the different textures.

Jigsaw Puzzles   Older children look forward to working more complicated puzzles, all the way up to extremely difficult jigsaw puzzles. They can work these by themselves or with friends.

Kids can make jigsaw puzzles, too. Pages from old magazines can be mounted on construction paper and then cut up.

Educational puzzles create the alphabet or the United States or the countries of the world.

You may want to consider a puzzle exchange with friends who have children near the ages of yours. Your children will get to try new puzzles for a few weeks, and their old puzzles will seem like familiar friends that need to be reworked once they return home.

Teach your kids to keep all the pieces to a puzzle together and to work only one puzzle at a time. (Since puzzle boxes sometimes tear easily and spill readily, keep puzzle pieces in a plastic bag.)

Three-Dimensional Puzzles
Rubik's Cubes and small metal puzzles can keep children occupied for hours at a time. They're good take-along toys as the kids accompany you on errands.

Word Puzzles
Puzzle books for children come in specialized themes or feature a specialized type of puzzle, such as jumbled-letter, crossword, and secret code puzzles. And with them, your kids will learn new vocabulary words, develop perception skills, learn to follow rules and puzzle protocols, and gain practice in spelling.

Art Puzzles
These puzzle types include mazes, connect-the-dots, and hidden pictures.

Riddles
Invest in a simple-to-read riddle book and let your children make up their own games as they quiz each other.

6 ▲ Animal Care and Training

Watching and playing with their pet will benefit kids more than watching Lassie on TV. Furthermore, the care and training of a pet can be a time-consuming activity that leaves little time for wondering what's on the tube.

Type of Pet   In addition to cats and dogs, you may want to consider these pets:

- *Fish.* Children can be taught and then be required to take on the responsibility of feeding the fish, cleaning the fish bowl, and maintaining proper water chemistry.
- *Birds.* Cockatiels and parakeets can be trained in amazing ways. Again, it should become the children's responsibility to clean the cage and supply fresh water and food.
- *An ant farm.* Although these sealed, self-contained units require no maintenance, children can learn from watching the ants at work.

Guidelines   Choose a pet suitable to the ages and levels of maturity of your kids, their temperaments, the area in which you live, and your

willingness as an adult to help shoulder the responsibility for this particular pet.

Keep in mind that kittens become cats, puppies
become dogs, bunnies become rabbits, and cute
little yellow ducks become big white birds! Ducks,
chickens, rabbits, and large animals are probably
best left to farms and homes with sufficient acre-
age.

Whenever appropriate, let your kids have a say
in choosing the pet. They will feel more responsibility for a pet they help to pick out.

Responsible Ownership   Give children
the primary responsibility for the care and training
of the animal. A pet will develop children's patience and compassion. A pet will teach them limits
of behavior. Furthermore, in the ongoing care of
and interaction with a pet, your kids will learn
about the need for proper medical care and preven-
tive health care, about the attributes of loyalty (and
that loyalty is a two-way street), about procreation
and birth, and about the need for practice and
more practice in developing habits and physical
skills.

Pet Visitation   You may choose a pet that
your children visit. The pet may be a horse
boarded at a farm a few miles from town, a special
animal in the petting zoo, which you have affec-
tionately named and consider to be "part of your
family" even though the animal lives elsewhere, or

an animal that belongs to a relative. Regular visits are a fun alternative to TV!

Consider taking your kids to a pet show, especially a show featuring their type of pet, such as a dog show, cat show, and so forth. They will get to choose their own favorites.

7 ▲ Scrapbooks

By working on a scrapbook—choosing items, organizing them, gluing them in, and so forth—children develop a sense of design, priorities, and likes and dislikes. Making a scrapbook requires creative choice and involvement with the subject matter, neither of which are required in depth by television.

Personal Interests   Is one child a sports enthusiast? She might keep a scrapbook of photos and newspaper articles about her accomplishments or those of favorite sports figures.

A young child can create a scrapbook on a particular topic. Give him old magazines so that he can cut out pictures of airplanes, cars, flowers, horses, puppies, or any pictures he likes. After all, it's his scrapbook.

For "my house" scrapbook, your child can create rooms and choose different styles and items that she'd like to see in her dream home.

Christmas Wishes   Do you receive a lot of mail-order catalogs at your house? Let your children cut them up to create their own "biggest and best just-for-me catalog" filled with all of their favorite things. Pursue this activity as Christmas looms on the horizon. However, be sure to remind the children that just as you don't buy everything you see in catalogs, so you aren't going to buy them everything you find in their catalogs.

Special Events   One child may want to make a scrapbook devoted exclusively to a vacation or to a series of vacations. Another child may devote a scrapbook specifically to birthday or holiday celebrations. Or he may want to make a scrapbook about the family—with a section for each family member.

Contents   A scrapbook could contain any of these items:

- *Favorite photographs* with time, place, and people or objects labeled
- *Ticket stubs and programs* of events your child has attended as well as ones in which she has had a part
- *Newspaper clippings* related to your child or to events, friends, or community happenings that your child considers important or memorable
- *Items that mark special events,* such as the first baby tooth that your child loses, a name tag from a special event, a first airline ticket, a photocopy of your child's first paycheck, a

dried flower from the corsage your child is given before a special dance or party
- *Original creations,* such as poems or small pieces of artwork
- *Postcards* of places visited or places your child dreams of visiting someday
- *Ribbons, medals, and certificates*—"prizes" your child receives, certificates of membership, baptism, confirmation, and so forth
- *Special letters,* perhaps from noted public figures, beloved relatives, or a respected minister or priest

8 ▲ Music Practice

It's daily.

It's noisy—and sometimes discordant.

And sometimes, it seems like forever before one senses a degree of progress.

But music practice does more than give a child a level of skill in reading music and playing an instrument.

Lessons   Music practice

- develops discipline of the daily variety. Insist that your child agree to practice if you are going to pay for lessons, and that your child practice without complaint. Not everything in life is fun all the time, and not everything in life can be accomplished in a day. Both are valuable lessons.

- should be scheduled, generally on a daily basis. The scheduling of practice time teaches time management.

- encourages a child to set goals and to break them down into subgoals to accomplish them. For example, the child's goal may be to learn to play the entire score of "The Entertainer."

A subgoal may be a certain scale or "run" or segment of the piece.

- is self-rewarding and self-reinforcing. A child generally knows when he plays the wrong note, squeaks or squawks, or misses a fingering. Repetition of a task until it is performed successfully builds patience, persistence, and a sense of personal accomplishment.
- enhances eye-hand coordination (and in some cases, eye-hand-and-foot coordination).
- helps your child discover more about potential, inherent traits and abilities, and the correlation between practice and performance.

Learning to play a string, wind, or percussion instrument prepares your child for interacting with others in a band, an orchestra, or a musical ensemble.

Vocal training is a suitable activity for children. Participation in a children's choir is a great learning experience.

Method   A new method called The Miracle teaches a child to play a keyboard linked to a computer: it provides personalized reinforced instruction. Music practice and lessons have never been so fun or so easy!

Teachers   The value of a music teacher cannot be overlooked or replaced, however. A music teacher can develop special talents or help a child overcome bad habits. A teacher can also work with a child to develop a musical ear, an appreciation for music of all types, and a knowledge of music history and theory.

Performances   Music lessons and practice seem to lead inevitably to music performance—the annual or semiannual recital. Through these performance opportunities, your child overcomes stage fright and develops skills necessary for appearing in front of an audience—skills that are readily transferred to giving a public presentation as an adult one day.

9 ▲ Watching

Kids should be observers of more than the animated box in the living room.

Bird Watching   Children of all ages can use a pair of binoculars to watch neighborhood birds, especially when nests are being built, eggs are hatching, and young birds are learning to fly. Help your kids identify birds of different types; develop their interest in the variety and unusual aspects of the natural world.

You may want to buy a book about bird species to teach the names of birds. Your children will quickly discover the differences in coloration and habits of the males and females of a species. You may also want to buy a bird-calling whistle for each child or a tape of different bird sounds. Log the names, times, and places of the birds your children spot.

You may want to put up a bird feeder, a birdbath, and a birdhouse for your backyard, patio, or balcony. Then the whole family can watch wild birds avail themselves of a meal and bath. Make your children aware of the migration of birds. They can make a car game out of spotting flocks of birds as they fly north in the spring and south in the fall.

Weather Watching Teach your children to read the weather signs in nature; they are just as interesting as the weather reports on television. Children can learn the names of clouds and the types of formations that frequently lead to snow, rain, or violent weather. Give each child a stint at being the personal family weather reporter.

Teach them to read a thermometer and a barometer, and place versions outside. Invest in a rain gauge and teach your kids to measure precipitation. They may want to keep a log of weather-watching activities—perhaps charting temperature, cloud conditions, and whether a day is sunny or cloudy.

Your kids may observe natural weather predictors apart from the phenomena in the skies —such as the growth of bark on trees, the distinctive chirping of insects, the behavior of animals before storms, and the growth of an outdoor animal's fur coat. Give your children the current *Farmer's Almanac* and see what interesting tidbits they glean.

Star Watching Your children can spend prime-time hours exploring the real stars instead of viewing the stars on prime-time television. You can get them started with an inexpensive telescope and a chart of the stars. You may want to include a moon calendar that shows the moon in its different phases every day of the year.

Learning about the stars gives your kids an appreciation for the vastness of the universe and the precision of the seasons as they come and go. They may want to keep a chart of daily sunrise and sunset times and notes about "falling stars," orbiting satellites, and other night-sky phenomena.

"Other" Watching   Just about anything can be watched. Position your young child's playpen in front of a sliding glass door with the drapes drawn so he can watch all of the doings of the yard or neighborhood. Animals can be watched as well as birds; look for squirrels in the trees or deer that come near the backyard for food in the winter. As you travel with your children, make "people watching" a part of your family activity. Of course, this doesn't mean staring.

10 ▲ Concerts, Plays, and Other Live Events

Let your kids experience the thrill of live performances.

Concerts or Recitals   Numerous community concerts are free, especially those for children. Many symphony orchestras have one concert a year to which the public is invited free of charge—perhaps a concert in the park or at a skating rink. Check the schedules at a nearby college or the local high school for performances by the school's band, orchestra, or choral groups. Your young musicians will not be dismayed that the quality of the performance may not be up to your trained-ear adult standards. They'll be fascinated that young people are performing the music.

Is a favorite performer coming to town? You may want to splurge for tickets. Be wary of rock concerts, however. They certainly aren't for young children. (In fact, I don't recommend them at all for children or young teenagers.)

If your children are learning to play instruments or show a special interest in one type of music, you may want to expose them to a concert featuring their instrument or favorite music. Colleges frequently hold recitals by seniors or graduate students. Small ensemble groups also perform regularly.

Many communities sponsor a children's series of concerts. Performers explain the music and display the capabilities of various instruments in an educational way for the young audience members. Children also learn about the etiquette of concert going.

Also encourage children to attend the recitals of friends. Let them learn to applaud as well as to perform. Attending a recital is one way of expressing friendship and providing moral support.

Churches frequently present musical programs —usually choir oriented—especially on Sunday evenings. Often the programs have a theme, such as patriotism, or are related to a holiday, such as Christmas.

Dramatic Performances   Churches, schools, and community theaters regularly present plays, musicals, pageants, and variety shows, many of which are suitable for family viewing. (If you have a question about the content of a show, call in advance.) In addition, some communities have a children's theater season.

Mimes sometimes frequent city parks or zoos.

Puppet shows always appeal to children.

Other Events   Although you may not think of them in the same category as a Broadway musical, circus acts offer drama and a high degree of showmanship. Take your kids to the circus.

Watch for traveling shows with characters your kids may recognize—such as the annual Sesame Street characters in concert or a Disney review performance.

Children are delighted at the antics of the Harlem Globetrotters—more show than athletic event. And an Ice Capades performance showcases skills on ice.

Children of all ages never tire of certain ballet programs, especially "The Nutcracker." Don't be surprised if you find your kids trying some of the moves they see the dancers make.

Many children are fascinated by a live performance of opera vignettes. They often sit spellbound at the power and potential of the human voice.

A live performance shows your children that mistakes and flubs are parts of real life. The perfection of television isn't the norm. This realization frees many children to take risks and to try their hands at new activities related to music and drama.

11 ▲ The Park

Discover the activities at a local park.

Lots to See and Do   Depending on its location and features, the park is a good place to investigate

- displays of artwork and craft items.
- ducks, geese, and swans swimming on the lake or pond. Take a bag of bread crumbs with you. (If your park doesn't have a pond, it may well have pigeons. They also enjoy eating what you bring.)
- merry-go-rounds, slides, large sandboxes, swings, and other playground equipment to which your children don't have access at home.
- plenty of wide-open space for running, skipping, flying a kite, or throwing a Frisbee.
- a zoo. Many parks have small zoos associated with them. In other cases, the park you visit may be primarily a zoo.
- a small ice-skating rink or perhaps a roller-skating/skateboarding cement surface or perhaps small amusement-park-style rides.

• people. Enjoy watching the grandmother pushing a pram, the grandfather dozing on a bench, the jogger huffing and puffing his way down the walk, the local group of guys playing softball, the young mothers with their children at the sandbox, the ice cream vendor with his pushcart, the skateboarders doing their tricks, the dancers practicing their moves, the child learning to roller-skate, the college kids studying while sunbathing, and the list goes on.

Live Action   The park is a good place for your kids to run and get rid of the pent-up energy of the day, and

• to greet friends who seem to frequent the park about the same time you do each day.
• to note the changing of the seasons.
• to watch birds and squirrels.
• to fly kites.
• to yell and scream as much as they want.
• to collect pebbles and leaves and twigs.
• to play group games and sports.

The park is a good place to go when home or the yard or the balcony or the patio is too small a place to play.

12 ▲ Sewing Projects

Because sewing involves a number of steps, your kids develop a wide range of skills:

- Making choices. Choosing a pattern and fabric and matching accessory items (such as buttons or trims) is one giant exercise in decision making and creativity.
- Following a prescribed set of instructions. As children learn to read and follow a pattern, they learn about sequencing.
- Doing work precisely. Sewing is a skill that challenges kids to do high-quality work and to learn when it's best or necessary to rip it out and try again.

Along the way, eye-hand coordination is developed. Perseverance is required. And the completion of a job well done (and an item of clothing or interior decoration) becomes a point of accomplishment that enhances self-esteem.

Sewing projects help children become aware of their bodies and likes and dislikes. Over time, they develop a personal concept of style, which they may express through what they sew.

The Basics   Give your kids sewing lessons or at least teach them how to use a sewing machine. Even if they don't become masters at handwork or sewing, they need to learn to use a needle and thread and to make simple repairs or alterations to garments: to repair a ripped seam, to put in or change a hem, to replace or reinforce a button, and to patch a garment.

Other Projects   Sewing can also include these projects:

- Lacing and weaving
- Needlework, embroidery, and cross-stitch
- Knitting and crocheting
- Quilting

Several easy, quick-to-finish projects are marketed so that your children may gain more immediate gratification.

Creative Outlet   Sewing provides a wonderful creative outlet for children. They can mix and match ideas, fabrics, and garments. Even children who don't enjoy sewing clothes may enjoy sewing doll clothes and accessories or stitching a new set of curtains or pillows for the bedroom. Boys often tackle unusual sewing projects, such as adding decals and emblems to a vest or jacket or recovering a bicycle seat.

Hours spent sewing are hours spent in a creative, productive, and fun learning process—something television can't offer.

13 ▲ Radio

Radio and television may seem like brothers, but in fact, they are more like distant media cousins.

Radio engages the imagination in a way that television cannot. Just ask a person who grew up listening to radio dramas. To be sure, the Shadow *does* know, and each person has a version of what falls out of Fibber McGee's closet!

Several stations periodically play radio dramas, and cassette-tape series of some of those old shows are available in many public libraries. If they aren't in yours, you may be able to convince your librarian to order them for you or to request them through interlibrary loan.

There's more to radio, of course, than music, news, and drive-time talk shows.

A Police Scanner   Children may listen to live action as it happens "out there somewhere" in the nighttime hours.

A Multiband Radio   Explore the programming of other countries. Encourage teenagers to analyze how European radio stations interpret and prioritize news events, comparing their coverage to the way the stories are told or covered by the local network affiliate.

A Ham Radio Set   Children enjoy talking to other children in faraway places just as much as adults enjoy talking to other adults in other states and foreign lands. Preparing for licensure as a ham radio operator can be a time-consuming, skill-developing, and highly rewarding task for older children or teens. The world truly is becoming a global village, one in which English is being spoken by an increasing percentage of the villagers. Teens can have enriching experiences as they exchange ideas and information with teens in other parts of the world.

Science Kits   In addition to listening to the radio, many children accept the challenge of making radio sets. With various science kits, a child may build a radio receiver.

Walkie-Talkies   Walkie-talkies are a variation on the radio theme. You may want to encourage your children to learn Morse code and to practice sending and receiving coded messages over small radio units connecting bedrooms within your home or connecting the bedrooms of other children in your neighborhood.

14 ▲ Bubbles, Kites, and Paper Planes

Bubbles, kites, and planes can be a part of make-believe play. Kids can explore the possibilities of story lines that include flying.

Bubbles   Send your children outside with a jar of bubble juice and a few large and small wands (including a plastic ring-style holder that connects a six-pack of aluminum cans), and watch them make and blow bubbles.

Various bubble-making devices on the market include a toy camera that blows bubbles through its "lens" and other equipment that creates strings of small bubbles. Some of the larger and more elaborate wands are packaged with booklets that tell how to make oversized and unusually shaped bubbles.

(Note: Small children should be closely supervised when blowing bubbles. Bubble juice isn't for drinking!)

Kites   Right along with bubbles in the arena of wind-play toys are kites. Visit your local toy store and you'll quickly conclude that kites aren't what they used to be. There are multiple kites and kites for trick flying. Some require quite a bit of skill; teenagers will be challenged!

Kites generally require some assembly. Kite making provides yet another exercise for kids in learning to follow instructions.

Make certain that your kids know kite-flying safety rules and that they have plenty of open space in which to fly a kite—far away from electrical wires, television antennas, and trees.

Paper Planes   Encourage your kids to try their hands at making paper planes. With certain kits, children can make fairly large planes. They can learn engineering at a very practical level as they build a plane and experiment with flying it.

Although they are expensive and definitely not for young children, motorized planes that are maneuvered either by guide wires or by remote control devices can teach various skills. Again, an open space is required away from crowds.

15 ▲ Typing Practice

Typing is a prerequisite to success in various fields, especially in the world of computers (including word processing, marketing, economic forecasting, scientific formulations, and statistical monitoring).

Furthermore, your budding high-school and college students will find good typing skills to be a lifesaver when they have to prepare term papers. Some students might even turn those skills into a part-time job or a way to help friends.

Learn the Right Way   Children are exposed to keyboards at an early age. That makes it even more important for them to learn to type accurately with good form that can lead to fast speeds.

Get a typing instruction booklet, and encourage your kids to practice. Daily. Without looking at the keyboard. It may take twenty minutes a day for six months before they become adept at typing. In the years ahead, your kids will thank you many times over for insisting that they acquire this skill.

What if You Don't Have a Typewriter?

Scour the flea markets. Look through newspaper ads. Talk to people in repair outlets that specialize in computers or typewriters. In other words, look for a bargain. Outdated computer systems and typewriters (manual, electric, and electronic) are frequently available for just a fraction of their original price. The keyboard unit you purchase may not be one you'd want to use for projects that need a highly professional look, but it can be great for learning to type.

Typing can be learned in the time it takes to watch one TV sitcom for one thirteen-week series of programs, most of which your children will not be able to recall by this time next year. Redeem the time.

16 ▲ Collection Building

Most children seem to be pack rats. Frequently, the "precious things" take on a certain similarity or tend to focus on a particular interest. Voilà! A child has a collection!

What's in It? A child can build a collection of virtually anything:

- Stamps
- Butterflies (or other insects)
- Rocks (highly polished or as found, cut or whole, gemstone or garden variety)
- Shells (exotic or beach fare)
- Coins (although this is frequently too expensive for a child's collecting, apart from pennies)
- Dolls
- Teddy bears (or stuffed animals in general)
- Old keys
- Stickers
- Postcards

Some children collect a certain type of figurine, such as clowns or horses.

Certainly, a valuable and useful collection is that of books, especially sets of favorite children's books.

Collections can be of the nature walk variety—feathers, leaves, or seed pods.

Many children collect cards, such as baseball cards or the relatively new cards of the astronauts.

Girls often collect charms for a bracelet or necklace. Boys frequently collect caps or T-shirts.

Christmas ornaments can be collected and displayed each year. Ultimately, the set can go with the grown child as he or she establishes a home.

Helpful Hints　　Emphasize the joy of the hunt more than the acquisition. Let your children have a good time searching for items on their own.

Focus on items that are fairly inexpensive. Ideally, children should use their own money, with some items coming as gifts from parents or other relatives.

Help kids identify an item that they truly enjoy using, looking at, or reading about. Try to find an item that will hold their interest for several years.

Building a collection gives kids a sense of accomplishment, of perseverance (finding that one last rare item), and it promotes a desire to conduct research into a particular area. In addition, your kids can sometimes learn about the financial aspects of collecting and dealing in collectibles. You can spur on the collecting interest by finding books about the items they are collecting.

Children should organize and display their collections. For example, they may put postcards, stickers, or baseball cards in albums. In some cases, they may have to be inventive.

17 ▲ Library Exploration

Your local community library has far more than books. Encourage your kids to explore the library fully. Take them there for an occasional outing.

Tapes   Ask about collections of audiotapes or videotapes. Sometimes you can find rare tapes of early television programs, special concerts, documentaries of special events in history, or science programs. Many times, these are unavailable in the video stores. The best news is that they can nearly always be checked out free or at a reduced fee. Sometimes viewing or listening rooms are available.

Music   Ask about the music section. Your children have little familiarity with records—those of the 33 rpm and 45 rpm variety that you once thought were the newest and latest in recording innovation. Explore the old-time greats with your kids. Share the oldie-but-goody music you liked as well as the records your kids' grandparents and perhaps even great-grandparents enjoyed. Broaden your kids' musical horizons.

Visual Aids   Ask about slides and other collections of visual material. Research an upcoming vacation or help your kids with projects about faraway places.

Computers   Many libraries have computers with a wide range of educational software packages for public use.

Periodicals   Browse through the periodicals section. You'll find many more titles there than at any newsstand. Look for magazines that specialize in an area of interest to your kids. Children's magazines are frequently available.

Nonfiction   Consider going to the library with a specific list of questions or topics for you and your children to look up together in the nonfiction section. Wander the stacks together in search of "the answer." Don't wait for a homework assignment. Be enthused about learning for learning's sake.

Behavior   Teach your kids library etiquette, such as how to move about quietly and to speak softly when making requests or asking questions. Show them where the restrooms and drinking fountain are located so they can use them on their own. Teach them how to request information from a librarian, how to use a card catalog (or other filing system), where to browse for certain types of books, and how to be a friend both to the librarian and to other patrons using the library.

Spending an occasional evening at your local library can be a relaxing, yet enlightening time for parents and kids alike. There's one thing a library has that television doesn't: quiet. It's an atmosphere your kids will benefit from experiencing.

18 ▲ Research Projects

Closely related to library visits are research projects. These can take on several forms for children. Always begin with their interests or questions. Stimulate their curiosity and then help them find answers on their own.

Resources Most questions or topics won't require kids to delve into all these resources. At other times, they may want to read entire books on a subject or take a course of sorts in a field.

Use Reference Books Find out what is said in books and encyclopedias. Consult a dictionary frequently. Teach your children to look up words they don't understand or know how to spell.

Use Maps When a nation is mentioned on the news or at a church missions conference or in a conversation, find it on the map. Discuss the importance of its location and note its proximity to other nations. Use a variety of maps to explore the culture, topography, and natural resources of the area.

Use Magazines   Become familiar with the *Readers' Guide to Periodical Literature* as a means of finding current information. Especially look for articles that have pictures or illustrations to further pique the curiosity of your kids. If the language of the article is beyond their reading level, paraphrase the information.

Identify Experiments   With science kits from archaeology to zoology, your kids can conduct experiments on their own or with friends. Be cautious, however, when it comes to chemistry sets, and always keep such kits out of the reach of young children.

Talk to Experts and Go on Field Trips Together If a child shows a special interest in a particular profession or topic, you may want to seek out a person in that profession and ask for a brief interview. Go with questions prepared in advance and written down for your reference during the interview. Ask about how the person does the job, what training was required to prepare for the job, and what he sees as the benefits of his work (both to himself and to society).

Search Out Special Public Exhibits, Museums, or Other Places of Interest   Don't overlook planetariums, botanical gardens, zoos, aquariums, historical museums, galleries, and special technology shows as places where your kids can find examples to look at and experts to talk to.

Travel   As you travel, stop by national monuments and parks and enjoy the programs available for public viewing. Your children can learn from these free exhibits and media programs.

Diversions   Research projects, of course, don't need to focus on academic subjects. Your kids may be most interested in pursuing sports trivia or looking up the answer to a question about a hobby. For that matter, a shopping trip can provide an exercise in comparison research as you and your kids look for the best buy (weighing such factors as price, quality, durability, serviceability, and so forth).

Family   Tell children about a family tree. They can discover their ancestors as well as learn more about the nation and continent where ancestors once lived.

19 ▲ Parlor Games

Turn off the TV game shows and get out the game boards.

What They Can Play   Teach your kids to play the familiar favorites, and occasionally play these games with them:

- Checkers and Chinese checkers
- Chess
- Monopoly (consider, too, the fairly new version of Monopoly for children)
- Card games (such as Rook, Old Maid, Fish, Authors, or 21)
- Scrabble or Scrabble Junior or other word games
- Trivial Pursuit (also with children's versions)
- Pictionary
- Other board games (such as Candyland, Uncle Wiggly, Chutes and Ladders, and Sorry!)

New games are being invented all the time. Periodically explore your local game store or toy shop.

When They Can Play   As you travel, consider taking along magnetic or pegged versions of checkers and chess.

Children can fill up spare minutes such as those in waiting rooms by playing a quiet game of Hangman or Tick-tack-toe.

What They Learn   Parlor games teach children that competition isn't always limited to physical skills or brute force. They also learn how to take turns, how to lose gracefully, how to work with a partner (in certain games) and, in some cases, how to reason mathematically or develop strategy skills.

20 ▲ Hide-and-Seek

By playing hide-and-seek, kids develop perception skills as well as gain a sense of control over play action (especially when they hide themselves or an object).

If you are playing along, or if your time for play is limited, make sure your children understand that they must respond to your call or designated signal. This is especially important if you are playing outdoors or in an unfamiliar location. Also make certain that at least one person stays put as a home base at all times. All participants should be able to find their way "home."

Just as much fun as playing the "human" version of hide-and-seek can be playing I Spy. A designated object in a room is selected as the goal of the game, and each person asks questions that lead to its identity.

Away from Home   As a travel game or a game to take along on a visit to a doctor's office or dental clinic, make a list of items in advance for your kids to look for during the excursion. (The list can be long or short, depending on the length of your trip. You may want to make a new list for each day of a multiday journey.) As a child spots items, mark those items off the list, or put the child's initials next to them. The goal of the game may be to find all of the items or to see which child finds the most items. The game takes your kids' minds off the length of a trip or distracts them from fear or concern associated with a trip to the doctor or dentist.

In the Neighborhood Another variation on the hide-and-seek theme is to send your kids out into the yard or neighborhood to find a list of items or note the location of various items. For example, ask them to make a note of something yellow, to describe where you can find the rose-bush with the most roses in bloom on it, to count the number of blue cars parked in your apartment complex parking lot, or to count the number of bird's nests in the trees on your block.

In Their Rooms Yet another variation on the hide-and-seek game is to send your kids into their rooms to find certain objects. This is an especially effective way to preface a demand that they clean up their rooms.

21 ▲ Creative Performances

Challenge your children and their friends to prepare a performance.

Play   Suggest one based on a holiday theme, such as Thanksgiving or the Fourth of July. Let your children

- write the play.
- design the costumes.
- create the props and sets.
- make up the programs.
- do fliers for distribution to family members and friends.
- design lighting and special effects (including selection of musical interludes).
- choreograph or block moves.
- conduct rehearsals.

This activity may take several days.

Variety Show   Encourage each child to work up an act.

Concert Your children may want to create a show based on their favorite songs and come up with their own choreography and lip-syncing performances of them.

Puppet Show Socks decorated with yarn and buttons will do for puppets. Again, children make up their scripts and develop their characterizations, sets, and special effects.

TV Show Given the technology of the age, the performance your kids and their friends create may very well be a videotape. Older children are adept at using camcorders, especially with adult supervision. Encourage them to develop a video script and then shoot it in sequence (to avoid editing) after carefully designing each segment and rehearsing it fully.

Parade Although not always considered a performance, a parade qualifies as an event that requires planning and showmanship and prompts audience applause. Suggest that your kids and their friends create a neighborhood parade to include all the children.

Neighborhood Fair Children can put together booths and invite the neighbors to admire their handiwork and artwork, view their collections, buy their cookies and cakes, and play their games (from darts to fishing with magnets for small prizes). Pets—in cages, of course—can be admired and judged in a pet show competition. Prompt your kids to come up with a way to make every entry a winner.

Competitions   Children can plan and sponsor a neighborhood, church group, or club tournament—a chess tournament or a swim meet, their own version of the Olympics (with such team sports as handball, and such individual sports as a fifty-yard dash), a marbles, jacks, or yo-yo competition, or perhaps a contest for mud castles. Again, prompt your children to find a way of applauding each competitor.

22 ▲ Nature Walks

Go for a walk. A walk provides a means of exercise and a release from the stress of the workday (including the workday spent doing housework). And a walk provides a time together for children and adults.

Talk   Notice things around you as you walk. Comment on them. Point out new or unusual things, including the blooming flowers, the branch that fell during the storm, and various signs that indicate a change of season.

You can also talk over the day. Explore what went on in your kids' lives even as you explore your neighborhood.

Visit with Neighbors   Pause to share ideas or news with those you find working in their yards. You'll probably come home with at least one new idea.

Take Note of Nature Where You Find It
Talk to the neighborhood dog. Watch the squirrels play in the trees. Observe the birds as they settle down for the evening. Pause to consider the ants

and beetles and butterflies. Call attention to the beauty of cloud formations or the glory of a sunset. Inhale deeply.

At times, you may want to draw conclusions or make comments about what you see on your walk. At other times, you may want to walk in silence and absorb the moment visually.

You'll find that your kids look forward to these times when they can count on being with you. They'll find comfort in exploring aspects of their neighborhood with you. And they'll especially enjoy a late-night walk as something unusual and exciting.

Walk in Other Areas   From time to time, take a walk through a community park. Or visit a local botanical garden or nature preserve. Try to visit such an area at least once a season. Notice the changes from visit to visit. Build into your kids an awareness of the beauty associated with each season.

Drive out in the country and walk along country roads, forest trails, or lakes and rivers. You'll return home feeling as if you've been on a mini-vacation, and chances are, your children won't miss the regularly scheduled programming of that night.

23 ▲ Journal Writing

Keeping a journal or a diary, making periodic entries, has several benefits for your children.

Your Children Develop Language Skills   They will become more adept at expressing themselves in writing and will probably find that writing becomes less a chore and more a delight. This is a chance for your kids to develop a style of written communication, to practice penmanship, and to feel a need for a greater vocabulary.

Your Children Record Comings and Goings, Accomplishments, and Activities   As children look back over a journal, they frequently have a sense of personal growth and of trends in their lives, even though any single day may seem fairly routine or boring. They may want to keep lists of books read, movies seen, places gone, and so forth.

Your Children Express Pent-up Feelings   The journals of children are frequently punctuated by bursts of anger, frustration, "puppy love" feelings, and great affection—all of which are part of the growing-up process. Putting these feelings in writing is a way of releasing them and channeling them outward in a positive way.

Your children may want to include personal sketches or artwork. They may want to write poetically at times.

A Journal Can Take Many Forms

1. *Diary.* Diaries are places to note feelings as well as events and activities.

2. *Dreams.* In a journal, a child can sort out recurring, disturbing, or frightening dreams.

3. *Lists.* Sometimes the lists can be of feelings, activities, names of friends and others encountered at school and play. Sometimes the lists can relate to goals and ideas and future plans.

4. *Questions.* The journal may include a section of questions that a child is pondering.

Permit your children to keep their journals personal and private. Don't snoop. If you are also keeping a journal, you may want to share a portion of it from time to time, which opens the door for your children to share theirs with you.

Emotions and ideas are best expressed. When they are retained, they can erupt into frustration, anxiety, worry, fear, doubt, or other types of distress. Journal writing allows kids something that television inhibits: the opportunity to create words and give voice to the inner self.

24 ▲ Model Making

Through model building, children

- learn to follow instructions. Models must be built in sequence.
- develop patience. Painted pieces must dry before they can be glued together; certain glued-together pieces must dry before they can be combined. The process can take many days.
- learn perseverance. When children stick with a task until it is finished, they reinforce habits of discipline. The completed projects build up self-esteem and confidence.
- develop small motor skills. Models require precision and manipulation of small pieces.

Cars and Planes   By making model cars and airplanes, children can learn about the working and design of the real things. In addition, they can learn about twentieth-century history as they make planes and cars representative of certain eras. (Models of planes and cars are yet another type of collection your children might want to build.)

Working Models   Children can build working models, such as a radio set, a robot that responds to commands, and a small pump that moves water.

Some types of construction sets can be used to make models of various types of machinery, such as cranes and elevators. Children can design, create, and then manipulate items they've constructed.

Science   With the Invisible Man and Invisible Woman kits, children can paint and then put together the organs of the body within a clear plastic casing. These models teach about anatomy and are useful in explaining certain medical treatments or physical ailments to children.

With models of skeletons of dinosaurs, children can create prehistoric creatures.

Joint Effort   Model building is an activity that parents and children can do together—assuming, of course, that you are wise enough to let the children assign labor to you. Let them make all the decisions about paint color and the positioning of decals. One of the best things a parent can do is to watch, applaud, and engage in conversation about the item that a child is making.

Provide a place where kids can work on models until they are completed. Make sure that other children keep their hands off the projects and don't interfere with the building process. And by all means, keep small model pieces and glue away from young children.

Once models are completed, display them. You may want to build shelves just for the purpose of displaying completed models.

25 ▲ Scouting and Other Groups for Children

Television is most often a solitary, passive activity for children. Channel your children's abundant energy, instead, into something that is active and that includes other children. Few alternatives are as valuable or as personally rewarding as membership in a Scouting organization.

Organizations   *Boy Scouts* and *Girl Scouts* prepare youngsters to feel a sense of responsibility for their communities, a sense of control over their own safety (both in the city and in the wild), and a sense of community with their peers that is positive, nonexclusive, and rooted in service.

Camp Fire Boys and Girls is another fine program, with virtually the same benefits as Scouts and an emphasis on WO-HE-LO . . . work, health, and love.

Royal Rangers is a church-based organization, as are several others you may want to explore for your children.

Growth   In virtually all of these organizations children may work their way up several ranks and earn badges, beads, or emblems along the way. Children learn specific skills useful throughout life, and they gain information that is enriching and builds self-esteem. They grow mentally, emotionally, and socially.

A Helping Hand Single parents frequently find that Scouting programs fill a niche for their children—providing a surrogate father figure for a young son or a mother figure for a young daughter. Get to know the troop leader; you'll want your children to belong to a unit in which the other parents are involved, and you'll want your children associating with children whose families share the values you consider important.

In addition to Scouting programs, you may want to learn about a Big Brother or Big Sister program. Although these organizations are purely aimed at fostering a relationship between a child and an adult—without tasks, achievements, and group activities—the programs are extremely valuable for children who need a positive friendship with an admired, older role model.

26 ▲ Practice Ranges

Practice may not result in perfection, but children certainly get a lot closer to it if they do practice.

Tennis Do you have a budding young tennis player in your family? Take her to a court that has a backboard against which she can hit . . . and hit . . . and hit. Buy a bucket of used balls from a local tennis club and let her practice her serve until she is satisfied with her performance.

Baseball Do you have a child interested in baseball? Save your quarters and let him spend time at a local batting range.

Golf Is your child learning to play golf? Both practice putting greens and driving ranges are available.

Bowling Is your child part of a bowling league? Many bowling establishments open their lanes for morning practice sessions, especially during the summer months, at reduced rates.

Firearms   Seminars sponsored by the local police and sheriff departments teach first and foremost that guns are *not* toys. They offer instruction in the safe and correct use of several types of firearms. Teens are frequently fascinated with guns, and these seminars direct that interest into a positive recreational skill, such as skeet shooting. Safe supervised firing ranges can be found in virtually every major city.

Archery   On the archery range, children can develop skills in accuracy and distance.

27 ▲ Conversation

Turn off the tube and talk to your kids. You may all be amazed at what you discover.

Don't have the television on during mealtimes. Use meals as a time for family communication. Linger over the dinner table and talk.

- Let every person share the foremost events of the day and explore related feelings and opinions.
- Discuss and evaluate events or experiences you've shared as a family.
- Plan future events and activities as a family.
- Share the news of the day. "Did you hear about . . . ?" and "Did you hear the news today that . . . ?" are opening lines for conversations that can be far-ranging in topic—from international political news to reports of new inventions and scientific discoveries to the announcement that a frequently used nearby road is being closed for resurfacing.

Spend a few minutes with each child at bedtime. Communicate on a one-to-one basis.

Beliefs and Values Conversations are opportunities for sharing, in an ongoing, natural way, your opinions, values, and beliefs. Don't wait until a crisis hits or a problem arises to share with your children what you believe to be fair and just behavior.

Feelings Conversations are opportunities to share with your family how you feel about events and activities. Let your children know when certain news makes you feel sad, happy, or confused. Let them see a full range of honest emotions from you and discover that talking about one's feelings is both acceptable behavior and a beneficial process.

Family Ties Conversations are ways in which your children will discover you as a person and each other as distinctive, uniquely gifted, and valued people. Share anecdotes from your past when they are appropriate. Let your children know that you have a reason for saying, "I can relate to that." You may want to share incidents from the lives of your parents and grandparents. Through conversations, children learn about their heritage —their family tree, their community history, their church denomination roots.

Debates Don't let your conversations dwell on topics that irritate or cause anger in one or more family members. A vigorous heated debate about politics should end with a friendly handshake. Debate is good for children to hear; encourage their participation. Make certain the debate is based on facts, however, and not just hunches. Encourage children to have evidence to support opinions. They will emerge from such conversations with lots to think about and a better developed ability to reason.

Humor   Conversations frequently erupt in laughter. Make jokes and amusing stories and anecdotes a part of your conversations. Family members that laugh together are rich indeed.
Converse

• as you travel by car.
• as you run errands around town.
• as you sit in waiting rooms.
• as you prepare meals together.
• as you work on home-related chores with your kids.

Your children will develop both listening and speaking skills and will gain in self-respect.

28 ▲ Seasonal Sports

Activity is a key word. Television offers action but not activity. Kids need to spend growing-up years in motion. Turn your sports fans into participants.

Fishing   Take them fishing. Teach them how to bait a hook, cast a line, and reel in a fish. Teach your children safety around the water. Some cities have small man-made lakes specifically designed for teaching and practicing fishing skills.

Snow-Related Activities   In winter, if you live in an area where it snows, encourage your children to turn off the TV and to go outside for sledding . . . cross-country   skiing . . . snowman building . . . or ice-skating (preferably at a supervised rink). Ice-skating, of course, can be a year-round activity. Many rinks are located in permanent structures, including shopping malls.

Water Sports   In summer, take your kids to the community swimming pool for lessons. Make certain that they learn to swim and learn safety rules around water. Summer is also a time when children go boating with adults or in their own rowboats. Again, make certain that they know the safety rules and wear life vests whenever they are in boats.

Leagues   Your children may want to join a community softball or T-ball league. The good news about T-ball is that every child gets to hit the ball and run the bases. Both boys' and girls' leagues are available just about everywhere. Call your local park service.

Soccer leagues are popular in most towns and cities. A number of large cities have basketball leagues, too.

Lessons   In addition to group sports, you may want to give your children lessons in tennis, golf, ice-skating, roller-skating, gymnastics, or another sport in which they express interest.

29 ▲ Art Projects

Art projects can keep kids busy any time of year.

Crayons and paper are musts for children. You may also want to supply a large pad of colorful construction paper, blunt-end scissors, glue, and an easel.

Consider these projects for your kids:

- Painting with water colors or tempera paints
- Working with clay, Play-Doh, or plaster kits
- Drawing with a Magnadoodle, Etch-a-Sketch, or other drawing kit
- Designing cars and other vehicles with a child's version of a T square and templates
- Making designs on paper with rubber or sponge stamps, stickers, and glitter
- Using a Colorforms kit for experimenting with designs and colors
- Designing clothes (with help from a kit)
- Making party decorations, centerpieces, or Christmas tree ornaments
- Learning the art of paper cutting or making items from papier-mâché
- Making small items of apparel or items for

home use with a small weaving kit or bead-craft kit
- Learning to knot string into macramé designs

Face Painting   Face paints are popular with children, as are kits that teach how to paint clown faces.

Sidewalk Painting   Large chunks of side-walk chalk come in a wide variety of colors so your children can create large-scale murals on a drive-way, patio, or sidewalk—all of which can be washed away easily.

Collages   Collages of photographs, of favorite things cut from old magazines, of discarded labels from cans and jars, of things brought home from nature are all possibilities. Works of art can be made from buttons, seeds, feathers, leaves, small strips of bark, and scraps of various types of wood.

Classes   Check with your local park service or community center about art classes that may be offered during summer months or on Saturdays.

Recycling   Kids can turn everyday dis-carded objects into useful items. For example, what could they do with glass jars? You may want to cut large detergent or cereal boxes to create holders for magazines or special school papers. Let children decorate them with paper, seals, and other "glitz." What could children create from egg cartons, milk cartons, or small pieces of fabric or wood?

Making a Place   Prepare an area of your home or yard where children can be as messy as they need to be as they create their works of art. Set aside a T-shirt that's just for painting, or make or buy an artist's smock to protect clothing. Teach children how to pick up after a project is completed.

Also designate a place for displaying their latest creations. It may be your refrigerator door or a bulletin board.

30 ▲ Treasure Hunts

Do your children ever come to you and moan, "We're bored"? Challenge them to create a treasure hunt. The point of the hunt, of course, is for children to move from clue to clue to find a hidden treasure.

"Treasure Isle" Let children take turns coming up with clues and hiding them for one another. Limit the "treasure isle"—perhaps designating the backyard, the living room, the apartment complex, or the block on which you live as the place in which all clues and the treasure must be hidden. Suggest that your children select the final hiding place first and then work backward to choose interim spots and create clues.

The treasure itself may be quite small (and may not even be something you'd normally think of as a treasure).

The clues may be done in rhyme or as riddles. Encourage the participants to be as clever as possible in their clues.

The hunt may involve a dozen clues and interim stops or only one or two clues and stops.

Party Fun A treasure hunt is an excellent birthday party activity (with the treasure being the cache of birthday presents hidden someplace in the house while the children pursue clues outside). A treasure hunt is also a good rainy day activity.

You may want to surprise your children with a treasure hunt of your own creation from time to time. Put out several clues that lead to a new accessory item, cassette tape, or other small gift item. Let them enjoy the thrill of the hunt.

31 ▲ Water Games

An alternative to TV viewing may be as close as the nearest water faucet.

Bathtime   Soap crayons are fairly new on the market; at bathtime, kids can turn the tile or fiberglass walls around the tub into an art canvas. Various water toys, including washable dolls, water pumps, and sponge building blocks, are fun and safe for bathtub play.

Toys   Squirt guns will always be a favorite. Some newer models are creative in design—trumpeting elephants and long-necked ostriches, among others.

Water toys, such as waterway transportation systems that accommodate toy boats, are popular with children.

The Garden Hose   Garden hose "battles" and sprinkler play serve double duty in the summertime. The kids get cooled off, and the lawn gets watered.

Pool Play   If your kids have access to a swimming pool, they can swim with fins, learn to use a snorkel and goggles, and play with inner tubes. A net across a pool sets up a game of water volleyball for older children and teens. Water polo is a great group activity in a swimming pool. Children enjoy playing Simon Says or Follow the Leader in the pool: if one child does a certain jump or dive, the other children must follow suit. Make certain they take swimming lessons and learn about water safety rules.

Sports   Children are enthusiastic about waterskiing, rafting, and boating. Make certain they wear life vests when in a boat and they are reminded frequently of the rules for boating safety.

Carwash   You might turn washing the family car into a water game. It won't be such a chore if kids know it's OK to get soaked and have a little fun at the same time.

32 ▲ Exercise

Even beyond the playing of sports and engaging in physical activity is exercise. Although you may think that children are always on the go, the reality is that a decreasing percentage of our nation's children qualify as being physically fit. While parents are jogging or working out at a gym, their children are frequently at home mesmerized by the family television set.

Foot Power   Whenever possible, encourage your kids to run or skip. Let them run ahead of you for a hundred yards and then run back to you. It's a great way for them to release pent-up emotions, and running-jumping-skipping children tend to sleep more soundly, too.

Invite young children to go jogging with you occasionally. Parents and teenagers can race-walk, jog, and run together.

Jump to It!   Buy your kids jump ropes. If they become restless or fidgety at the lack of activity, suggest that they go jump up and down a couple of dozen times.

Moving Indoors   What about those cooped-up days of winter? Invest in a minitrampoline for your house, and let your kids jump to their hearts' content. Suggest to your young teenager that she ride your exercise bike while she's talking with her friends on the phone.

33 ▲ Creative Writing

Making up stories is an alternative to watching the stories that others have written for television.

Writers learn by writing. As your kids write, they'll learn more about the fine art of storytelling, about how to express themselves creatively, and about the differences in literary genres.

Poetry   Challenge your young child to try his hand at writing a poem. Challenge your teen to compose her own rhythmic rhyme. Bear in mind that poetry is meant to be read. Periodically have a reading hour with your family in which each member shares something aloud, preferably a personal composition.

Songs   Challenge your child to make up the lyrics and tune of a song and to sing it. Challenge your teen to notate the song and give it harmony. (They'll be even more successful at notation and harmony, of course, if they've had music lessons.)

Scripts   Challenge your children to write a play, including ideas for characterization, settings, costumes, and lighting or special effects. It's just one short step from a play to a teleplay. Challenge them to write video scripts for favorite TV characters.

Give them an opportunity to perform the play with friends or other members of your family.

Challenge your children to write a script that ties together—in a creative and fast-paced way—the slides you took on your last vacation.

Word Plays   Challenge your kids to write riddles or haiku word pictures or a series of Hebrew-style proverbs. (If you don't know what haiku is, or the rudiments of Hebrew-style proverb writing, embark on a research project.)

Computer Literacy   If your children have access to a computer, they can practice writing on it. Typing skills will be enhanced along the way. In fact, you might insist that they spend as much time writing on the computer as they do playing games.

Much of "school writing" is limited to essays. Writing at home is a different type of activity that gives wings to creativity.

34 ▲ Memory Work

Memorizing can be an activity with rich dividends. Your children will be far more adept at learning lines for a school play or pageant and will become more comfortable speaking aloud in front of others. Self-confidence and self-esteem will grow as they see that they can commit something you consider important to memory.

The passages children memorize enrich their thought life. The passages can give rise to new ideas, provide comfort in times of crisis or sorrow, and be a part of thought processes as they weigh a decision.

What to Consider   Challenge your children to memorize some of the following:

- Tongue twisters
- Poems (Learning " 'Twas the Night Before Christmas" is the ultimate challenge for many young people!)
- Famous cultural or historical documents (such as the preamble to the Constitution or the Gettysburg Address or the "We Believe" statement of your church)

- Speeches from famous plays—for example, Hamlet's "to be or not to be" monologue
- Scripture passages—such as the Twenty-Third Psalm, the Ten Commandments, or the beatitudes
- Proverbs and wise sayings
- Prayers that are the cornerstone of your faith (such as the Shema or the Lord's Prayer)

Challenge your children to learn all the verses to "Jingle Bells," your favorite Christmas carol, or a favorite hymn. Teach them the lyrics to songs that you enjoyed as a child or teen.

How to Do It   Teach children to break down a passage into short segments and to build one passage upon the next like building blocks.

Encourage them to repeat and repeat and repeat a phrase or passage in committing it to memory.

Give children an opportunity to rehearse what they have learned before you in a nonthreatening atmosphere.

35 ▲ Rest

Teachers frequently complain that students are too tired to concentrate in class. One of the foremost reasons is that they've stayed up too late watching television.

Get Sleep   Insist that sleep has priority over a TV program. With the occasional exception of a special program, set a bedtime for your kids and stick with it, no matter what's on, how many other children will be watching the show, or how exciting your kids are certain a program will be.

Television programs frequently stimulate children and put them in a "hyper" mode mentally and emotionally, which makes sleep difficult. Turn off the television set well in advance of bedtime.

Reduce Noise   Many families are becoming increasingly noise weary. After a busy day of traffic, construction sounds, city noise, or school playground noise—with all the attendant bells and crashes and honks and clanking—home should be a place of quiet. Create a peaceful atmosphere in your home by turning off the tube.

Nap   Get children to take naps or have quiet times. Send them to bed with a book or puzzle and insist that they rest quietly for a half hour. If they don't want to read or work a puzzle, encourage them to daydream.

Daydream   Daydreaming is beneficial for children. It allows them to

- try on different roles for themselves—envisioning themselves in various places and positions and careers and, in the process, discovering what is comfortable and what is uncomfortable as they think things through.
- make up creative stories—including dialogue with imaginary friends or among imagined characters.
- project their futures—weighing choices, setting goals, and mapping out plans for reaching those goals.
- recall favorite memories.

The child who is able to daydream is a child who is rarely bored.

Pray   Encourage your kids to use rest time or before-you-go-to-sleep time to pray. It is also a good time to take a mental vacation—to concentrate on happy places and events.

Consider rest time to be good for the bodies and the souls of your children.

36 ▲ Craft Projects

By completing quality craft projects, children develop a sense of self-worth, of accomplishment, of pride in a job well done. Craft projects build the abilities to follow instructions and to put objects together in a way that is structurally sound and aesthetically pleasing. Craft projects stimulate creativity. And they give you opportunities to spend quality time with your children.

Kits Children can have fun with these kit activities:

- Building a birdhouse or a bird feeder or a birdbath
- Making and decorating a doll house, including simple pieces of furniture or accessories
- Making small wooden toys for a younger brother or sister
- Growing crystals
- Making an origami masterpiece or putting together an architectural paper model

Woodworking Junior carpentry kits are readily available, with tools scaled down for small hands, so that boys and girls may build things with wood and learn how to use a hammer, saw, drill, screwdriver, and other household tools. One of the simplest and easiest things they can learn to build is a rectangular step stool—a practical item that requires several different woodworking skills and principles.

Other Ideas Suggest some of these projects to your kids:

- Stringing beads together in unusual patterns to create necklaces and bracelets, using plastic or wooden beads
- Making molded figures from plaster and then painting them—for example, making a nativity set
- Lacing shapes together to create purses, key holders, and eyeglass cases
- Decorating clear plastic or wooden boxes with painted designs or glued-on shells, party glitz items, buttons, or other items of their choosing
- Stenciling fabrics and painting or stitching decorative emblems to T-shirts, sweatshirts, or tennis shoes
- Pressing flowers (and leaves) and using them to create stationery

Gifts Craft projects can be turned into meaningful and much appreciated gifts for grandparents, aunts and uncles, or teachers. When they spend time making a craft project that they give away, kids learn the true meaning of a "gift of time" and learn to value more highly the hand-made gifts they receive.

37 ▲ Bicycling

Bicycling helps children acquire balance. They get a sense of control and power as they choose where to pedal and how quickly. As your children exercise, they explore the neighborhood and spend time with other children.

Mechanical Device   A bicycle is very often a child's introduction to the way mechanical devices work. Realigning a bicycle chain, inflating a bicycle tire, and adjusting a bicycle's brakes can be good opportunities for teaching the basics of vehicle maintenance and repair.

Personal Choice   A bicycle is also a means of personal expression. With so many models on the market, the selection of a bicycle to a child is a little like the selection of an automobile to an adult. Go with your child as he looks at bikes, tries them out, and finally settles on a favorite. Teach him how to comparison shop for a bike and how to weigh various factors in deciding what makes a bike "good." Discuss the bicycle accessories, and allow your child to choose them or to purchase them from money he earns or saves from an allowance. He'll treat his bike with greater respect and take better care of it if he has a vested interest.

Traffic Know-How   A bicycle is your child's introduction to traffic safety. From an early age, teach him to wear a helmet and pads for his elbows and knees. Insist that he wear shoes. Crashing is a normal part of bike riding. Do what you can to protect him from serious injury. Above all, teach the rules of the road when it comes to cycling: how to signal, where to ride and, as he gets older, how to ride safely in traffic.

Family Outings   Bicycling is something you may want to do as a family. It's a great way to unwind together and to explore your city on an early Saturday morning. You may want to take your bicycles with you on family vacations.

38 ▲ Chores

It might be making the bed or changing the sheets on Saturday morning.

It might be cleaning out the bird cage or changing the puppy's water daily.

It might be dusting the furniture or pushing the vacuum sweeper in the hall once a week.

It might be mowing the lawn or raking leaves.

It might be scouring the bathtub.

It might be loading or unloading the dishwasher or setting the table for supper each night.

It might be emptying the wastepaper baskets.

Lots and lots of activities can qualify as chores. Chores are activities that are scheduled, assigned, and periodic (generally daily or weekly). And the scheduled assignee is 100 percent responsible for them.

It's Routine Doing chores should be part of kids' routines. Unless they are sick or out of town, they should be responsible for doing their chores without being asked and, generally speaking, without being compensated.

It's a Learning Experience   What do your kids gain by doing chores?

- They develop a sense of family responsibility.
- They learn personal discipline.
- They become aware of what it takes to create a clean, orderly, smooth-running home.
- They acquire housekeeping or yard maintenance skills.
- They learn that division of labor is the best way to get a major task accomplished, and that housekeeping or yard keeping work is not the sole or inherent responsibility of either Mom or Dad.

It's All in the Attitude   Insist that they do chores cheerfully and willingly. You'll be helping them gain a positive attitude that will carry them through a number of tedious and thankless tasks in life.

Periodically rotate chores so that children don't get stuck doing the same chore year after year.

And finally, insist that privileged activities—such as watching a favorite television program—cannot be pursued until chores are finished.

39 ▲ Map Making

Teach your children to read maps and to make maps. And then challenge them to map out their lives.

- Make a map of a room. Teach them how to measure and how to accurately record the sizes of objects.
- Make a map of your house or apartment. More measuring is involved. Your children may see home from a new perspective. If you live in an apartment complex, show them how the various apartments fit together to form a unit or floor.
- Make a map of your neighborhood. Locate key features. Introduce yourself to neighbors as you explain that your kids are making a map of your neighborhood and that you need to know how to label their house on the map.
- Make a map of your town. Obviously, a lot of details may be omitted. Ask your children to include the things significant to them.
- Make a map of school. They will feel comfortable starting a new school if you visit it first and make a small map of it for them to study.

- Make a map of your church or synagogue. Teach the correct names of various parts of the building.

Take your children with you to your place of employment some Saturday afternoon or evening and let them make a map of your office or work area.

Accuracy   Map making encourages children to note details and distinguishing characteristics. The more your children mature, the greater the detail their maps should convey. A map also teaches them about directions, distances, and the need for accuracy in projects based on mathematical calculations.

Innovation   As your children write creatively, they may describe an imaginary town or island with stories about various characters who live there. The town could be set in another era and perhaps even in an imaginary country. Maps will help them clarify the make-believe community, city, or nation. Even stories about families are frequently written with a greater depth of detail if children first draw the floor plan of the make-believe family's home.

Route Finding   As you take family vacations, let your children take turns at being navigator. Teach them how to read road maps and how to map out a desired route. (They will ask far fewer "when will we get there?" questions.) If you have the privilege of traveling by plane with them, familiarize them with air route maps.

"You Are Here"   As you shop in malls, enter unfamiliar high-rise buildings or office complexes, or visit tourist attractions, consult the maps near entrances or elevators. Show your children how to get bearings in a strange place and which way to turn once they discover the "You Are Here" point on the map.

Global Perspective   Provide a globe. When you hear about events in the news, look up the locations of various nations and states.

Spatial Sense   Maps give kids a sense of "space" and of control over their environment. Television rarely depicts the real world in any spatial sequence. A program may readily hop from London to Los Angeles with one swift cut. Furthermore, television often depicts home settings that are far more spacious, with far more levels, than are typical of the homes of most viewers. The real world is a world of spatial reality. Put your kids in touch with it.

40 ▲ Church

Participate in a church regularly. Make attendance a part of your family's weekly routine. If your particular church doesn't have a program aimed at communicating with children, either start one or find a church that has one.

Children and the Faith   The following activities are suitable for children:

- Church-related social functions. These include annual picnics, after-church social hours, and children's outings and day camps.
- Programs designed especially for them. Children's speakers, clowns, balloon sculptors, puppeteers, and stunt skateboarders have been known to visit churches and synagogues to convey religious messages.
- Services in which missionaries speak or show slides or videotapes. Tales of faraway places always intrigue children.
- Musical programs, especially pageants that include costumed actors and actresses.
- Programs in which a well-known athlete is the guest speaker.

Youth Group Most denominations and most churches have a youth group. Encourage young people to participate fully. Go along occasionally as a sponsor or chaperone.

Many churches have youth choirs. Kids will learn about music and the church. And this group activity teaches social and interpersonal skills.

Some churches sponsor Scouting groups, have Bible study times (catechism training, vacation Bible schools, and so forth), or hold fairs and parties just for children. Point your kids to these non-TV opportunities for fun and fellowship within the context of faith.

Encourage your teenager to work in the church nursery or to teach a church school class for younger children. Help your teen study the lesson and prepare graphic displays and activities appropriate for the age of participants.

41 ▲ Listening

Earlier, we addressed the idea of establishing an atmosphere of peace and rest in your home. This chapter emphasizes the need for kids to develop listening skills—something they can't do with the TV blaring in the background.

Music   Listen to music with your kids. Don't just have it on as background noise. Acquaint them with truly great compositions. With repeated exposure, they will anticipate certain musical phrases and passages.

Outdoors   Listen to the sounds of the night together. Sit out on the porch, balcony, stoop, or deck, and take in the night sounds. They may be city sounds: sirens, honks, and other noises. If you live in the suburbs or in a rural area, listen for the insects; learn to identify them by the sounds they make. Listen to the wind in the trees.

From time to time, challenge your kids to sit near you and then to close their eyes and identify as many different sounds as they can. Make it a game. If you're in the park or other outdoor location, listen especially for the songs of birds. If you're in the zoo, close your eyes and listen to the sounds of various animals.

Other People   In conversations with your kids, emphasize the need for developing good listening skills. They can't remember what you tell them to bring home from the corner market if they don't first listen to what you say. Quiz them—in an informal way—on what they remember from plays, sermons, or radio news reports.

Listening is a skill your kids will need all their lives. The better the skills, the better their chances of success at whatever careers or projects they undertake (including marriage!). Rather than "listen" to TV, encourage them to listen to life.

42 ▲ Letter Writing

Encourage each child to adopt a pen pal:

- A friend with whom letters are exchanged across the neighborhood
- A child in a foreign land
- A soldier
- A cousin who lives in a different city or state

Your child will develop language skills as well as a sense that the world really is a small place.

What to Write   Offer a few ideas about what to write: (1) friends, (2) family, (3) holiday customs, (4) sports, (5) favorite pastimes, (6) pets, (7) activities, (8) school, (9) books, and (10) goals in life. Encourage your child to ask questions, too.

Others to Write   In addition to ongoing correspondence with a pen pal, encourage your children to

- write letters of encouragement to friends who become sick or hospitalized.

- write letters to grandparents (or parents) who may live far away.
- write a thank-you letter for each present received.
- write to their member of Congress, senators, governor, state legislator, and to the president of the United States. Your children may tell the official that they are praying for him or her, that they appreciate the work that the person is doing for the good of our nation, and then close by asking a question or two. They may ask for a photograph of the leader.
- write to athletes, astronauts, and other people your children admire. They need only say, "I admire the work you do!"
- send postcards to friends while on vacation.

Your children will enjoy getting mail addressed exclusively and personally to them. To receive letters, however, one must also be willing to write them.

43 ▲ Room Cleaning

Children aren't born knowing how to clean. They must be taught how to vacuum, dust, clean windows, remove spots, and scrub bathroom surfaces. Children must be taught how to make a bed, hang up clothes, and pick up objects. And they can learn these skills at an early age, most effectively by working alongside you as you clean.

Orderly Living   Children aren't born with a well-developed sense of order. That, too, is learned. They aren't necessarily slobs or disobedient in having messy rooms. They may not see value in living in ordered rooms. To put rooms in order, however, they need sufficient space, shelving, pegs, hangers, baskets, stackable units, drawers, and so forth for the sorting and organizing process.

A desk for each school-aged child is recommended. That's the ideal place for doing homework, working on craft projects, and storing personal papers.

Once children have experienced living in an ordered world, they prefer it. They draw a sense of comfort from knowing where things are. They like the control of getting a toy, using it, and returning it. Children who are accustomed to being clean and living in clean surroundings are more comfortable with clean; it simply feels better to them.

Room Rules You can insist that kids not eat in their rooms to reduce the potential for messiness and staining. You can require them to make their beds each day and to put dirty clothes into laundry hampers. You can also insist that they keep any pet cages cleaned out on a daily basis.

Organization Teach them how to organize clothes and personal things, and how to set up files and binders for keeping things readily accessible. Boxes, baskets, and stackable units are helpful. Everything from magazines to underwear to paper clips can be separated and sorted. A certain amount of organization also saves time in getting ready for school or church.

Trash Days From time to time, join your kids in deep cleaning. These trash-out, mattress-turning, moving-all-the-furniture-away-from-the-walls days are great times of discovery. Your kids will be delighted to find the missing "something" that slid through the cracks or got wedged where it didn't belong.

44 ▲ Decorating and Remodeling

Children can help you with decorating and remodeling projects around your house or apartment, and they will be especially interested if those projects involve their rooms.

Teach your teenager how to make curtains, throw pillows, and perhaps a slipcover or bedspread.

Show your teen how to put up a shelf, paint the trim around the windows, and paint or wallpaper a wall (and perhaps add a wallpaper border).

Explore with your kids different ways to arrange their rooms. Ask them periodically to help you rearrange other areas of your home.

Fixing Up While Growing Up   Working around the house, puttering in the family workshop, and fixing things up are activities children should experience during growing-up years. Too often, however, parents are busy while children are immobile in front of the TV. Turn off the tube and invite their participation, even if the project takes longer. Count it a learning process for them as well as quality time spent together.

Family Projects   Projects that involve the entire family—such as clearing a patch of ground, relandscaping, or building a deck—add value to your piece of real estate and to your lives. Invite your kids to record handprints or footprints in the newly poured cement (under your supervision, of course).

Neighborhood Projects   If you live in an apartment complex, or a suburban neighborhood, you may want to join with neighbors for a remodeling or upgrading of your entire neighborhood. Explore ways in which you can make your immediate neighborhood a more aesthetically pleasing area. Fix things that are broken. Sponsor a youth art contest and allow young artists to paint original works over the present graffiti. Plant a few trees or bushes (especially those of the low maintenance variety).

Share the work as evenly as possible. The more people join in the process of repair, the less damage is likely to occur in the weeks and months ahead. Above all, involve your children. Let them contribute both ideas and working hands. They'll have a sense of community involvement and accomplishment and, with that, a sense of community responsibility.

45 ▲ Gardening

Give your kids a plot of earth they can call their own.

- It might be a sandbox that becomes a "dirt box."
- It might be a windowsill garden box just outside the bedroom window.
- It might be several rows in the backyard that are turned into a family vegetable garden.
- It might be a designated flower bed.
- It might be a few small containers for growing herbs.
- It might be a large container on the balcony or deck.
- It might even be a small "greenhouse" kit.
- On the other hand, it might be an acre of the family farm.

A Learning Adventure   Let it be a place where your kids can

- plan what they want to grow and prepare the soil for that particular crop.

- plant a seed and watch it sprout and turn into a plant.
- learn about cultivation—the need of all growing things for water, nutrients (fertilizer), weeding, pruning, and a pest-free environment.
- learn to identify the parts of a plant and the various stages that a plant goes through in developing its fruit.
- learn when to pick ripe produce and, after harvest, how to clear the plot of earth and prepare it for the next crop.

Whether growing flowers or vegetables, herbs or cacti, your kids will learn more about the processes of life, the foods they eat, and themselves as tenders of the earth.

Furthermore, gardens require nearly daily care. Weeding, watering, and harvesting are activities that build a certain amount of discipline and consistency.

In this day when environmental issues are at the forefront of our thinking, what better way to teach your kids how to be caretakers of the earth than to give them a little bit of earth to take care of!

46 ▲ Homework

Right next to "clean your room" in the Groan Department is a parent's insistence that children "do homework."

A Priority   Homework should always take priority over television viewing. In fact, it should be done first and done accurately . . . neatly . . . completely . . . and creatively . . . before the television set goes on. On most nights, that should just about preclude TV watching all together.

Don't let them take homework shortcuts to get to the TV set on time. Insist that they give best efforts to homework. Instill a desire in them to go beyond the assignment and to do something extra —to learn a bit more, try an extra problem, go for the extra credit assignment, study a little harder, or be as creative as possible in presenting the assignment. In the real world, that approach to work wins the promotion or launches a new company.

Putting homework as a priority before television not only ensures that homework will get done, but it

- sends a signal that you consider school to be the most important item on their agendas.
- compels your kids to engage in a version of time management.
- mirrors the real world—at least the world in which work must be done so the bills can be paid before play can be enjoyed fully.
- instills in them a habit of enjoying the processes of life (the homework) as much as the rewards (the desired TV show).
- establishes the idea that life inevitably has choices and that not everything they want to do in a day is always possible.

Don'ts and Do's
Don't nag your kids about homework. Expect it to be done as a matter of obedience.

Don't agree with them when they moan about having a lot of homework. Let them know you feel they are capable of accomplishing a great deal. "Just think. You'll be even smarter by morning!"

Do help with homework when they hit a snag. That does not mean you do the homework for them. Talk out the problems with them. Show them how to work a problem or research a topic or solve an equation or look up an answer. Periodically ask your kids to explain what their homework is all about. You'll gain new insights into the world that they face every day.

47 ▲ Creating Special Places

Children love to create and then spend time in special places all their own.

Outside and Inside   Work with them to create at least one outdoor and one indoor space primarily for their benefit. Outdoors, that might be a fort, a tree house, or a playhouse. A gazebo or a cleaned-out storage shed can be converted into or designated as a place just for play. Make certain that your kids can come and go from the place at will without danger.

Indoors, the secret place might be a converted closet, the space under a card table or dining table, or a large box turned on its side. The space need not be permanent—it can come and go as you and your kids desire—and it need not be fancy. A pup tent in a child's room may be an ideal permanent secret space to which she can retreat for moments of being "invisible" to the rest of the family. For the young child, a quilt on the floor or a playpen can be the designated private space—a convenient and portable one that can move from room to room as Mom or Dad goes about family chores.

"Worlds" of Their Own In addition to child-sized spaces, kids can create "worlds" using blocks, Legos, Tinker Toys, and other construction sets. These worlds are occupied by dolls, paper dolls, miniature figurines, and imaginary friends. Toy trucks and cars roam freely on imaginary streets.

Your kids can build an entire city around a train set—positioning and repositioning buildings and designing new routes in and around table legs and under a corner of the bed.

They can occupy a hallway and turn it into a fun house filled with pillows and rubber balls and stuffed animals—a place to curl up on a rainy day and make up scary stories when the lights are turned off and the hallway is plunged into near total darkness.

Perhaps you have a basement or an attic with a small space for your older child's or teen's use. That can be just as valuable as adding another room to the house, especially if the teenager shares a bedroom with a younger sibling.

48 ▲ Group Lessons

Permit your kids to participate in a learning group of their own choosing apart from the formal school structure:

- A gymnastics class
- A ballet class
- A tap dancing class
- An art class
- An aerobics class
- A baton-twirling class
- A cheerleading class
- A drill team class
- A consumer-awareness class
- A self-defense class
- A cooking class
- A series of drama lessons offered in the neighborhood park
- A class that teaches good manners and social graces
- A choir
- A band
- An orchestra

Aims The group class may be aimed at helping children with physical conditioning, skills development, or psychological coping mechanisms.

The group class may be designed to help kids put an end to a destructive habit, provide skills and support for overcoming an addiction, or put to rest a hurtful experience. It may be a therapy group.

The group may be directly related to your church—a Bible study group or another type of instructional class.

Group Interaction Your kids will benefit from the interaction with others and the general atmosphere of give-and-take, questions and answers. They'll be comforted to know that other children start out just as uncoordinated, ill-equipped, uninformed, or emotionally bruised as they may be. They'll learn the therapeutic value of group process. They'll learn a new skill, generally at a less expensive price for the parents. And above all, they'll be participating in life rather than watching it go by.

49 ▲ Computer Work and Play

Your kids probably think that computer games are the next best thing to television. Indeed, on the distant horizon one can envision the day when computers and high-density television sets will allow for interchangeable software.

For now, you can rest assured that most of the skills they acquire by playing computer games are good ones. Eye-hand coordination, quickness in decision making, and a certain amount of reasoning skills are enhanced.

Problems The problems with computer games generally fall into two categories:

First, Children Frequently Are Allowed to Play the Games to the Exclusion of Other Activities If children are allowed to play computer games too much, they suffer the same problems as children who sit too close to a television set for too long. The eyes and bodies suffer strain, and the children become isolated from other people. The "play" on the computer is prescribed rather than child-created, just as with television. (The difference is that television is a completely passive activity, whereas computers involve interaction.)

Second, the Content of Some Games Is Undesirable Learn enough about a specific computer game to know if it is in line with the values you are trying to instill in your kids. Some games require violent killing or total wipeout of enemy forces—values you may not want to reinforce.

Assets Computer software extends far beyond games, of course, to top-quality educational programs. Among the most popular are "Where in the World Is Carmen Sandiego?"—an educational program that teaches world geography—and "Where in Time Is Carmen Sandiego?"—an educational program that promotes a knowledge of world history. The programs are loaded with content, require skillful reasoning, and are fun to work.

Texas Instruments has designed programs to strengthen math, spelling, and grammar skills. And most word processing programs are useful for teaching kids to type and write.

Children get a real kick out of manipulating art programs, such as MacPaint for the Macintosh line of Apple computers. They can create party invitations, illustrate stories, and prepare artwork to impress friends.

Computers are with us to stay. Just don't let them monopolize all your kids' time to the exclusion of other valuable play and learning activities.

50 ▲ Videos

Videos are the "television of choice."

The Good   The good news about videos is that

- they are generally free of disruptive commercial messages.
- they can be stopped and started by the children, who retain some control, therefore, over the storytelling pace.
- they can be previewed by parents prior to viewing by children (and at hours that suit parents).

The Bad News   The bad news is that many movies made for children today are laden with violence—even those featuring popular cartoon characters. Monitor video choices closely. In fact, choose what your kids consume.

Most children enjoy a nonviolent video. They like action, to be sure, but they are just as concerned with characterization and a degree of fairness in the events portrayed. Not unlike adults, children like a good *story*. Children also enjoy a certain amount of long, slowly built suspense, something cartoons rarely attempt. Children like to see the good guys win and the bad guys punished. Children will often request permission to watch a good story again . . . and again . . . and again. Let them. They read and reread their favorite books. It's their way of learning a story.

The Guide The *Family Video Guide* edited by John H. Evans rates eight hundred recommended videos according to entertainment value —from a poor rating of 1.0 to an excellent rating of 4.0. To be included in the book, the movie may not have an R rating and must have limited or no gratuitous violence, drug use, illicit sexual behavior, or excessive use of bad language.

The guide gives the year the film was released, a brief description of its content, the Motion Picture Association of America classification for the movie (for example, G, PG, PG-13), the age of the youngest person to whom the film would appeal, the running time of the film, and whether it is in color or black and white. It provides a description of any "bad language" (according to definitions for mild crude, moderate crude, vulgar, and profane). The guide may be ordered through Movie Morality Ministries, Inc., 1309 Seminole Drive, Richardson, Texas 75080-3736.

▲ A Final Word

Children *can* live without a steady diet of television.

The weaning process, however, may be tough. Start by limiting television use an hour a day until you are down to no more than four hours a week of nonnews programming.

Choose with great care what your kids will see during those hours. Let TV become just another activity in their lives—not the primary activity, the preferred mode of entertainment, or the major preoccupier of their thought lives.

You may need to spend additional time with them as they make the transition from a television addiction to a full-life experience. You may need to teach them—and perhaps yourself—how to play, how to explore, how to converse with others, how to find pleasure in quiet yet stimulating, active yet nonaggressive activities. Make the effort! Both you and your kids will benefit.